The Happiness Book

The Happiness Book

◆

Volume One

Ten Daily Lessons
For Living A Life You Desire

Dr. Sandra Masters, D.D.

iUniverse, Inc.
New York Lincoln Shanghai

The Happiness Book
Volume One

iUniverse books may be ordered through booksellers or by contacting:

iUniverse
2021 Pine Lake Road, Suite 100
Lincoln, NE 68512
www.iuniverse.com
1-800-Authors (1-800-288-4677)

ISBN: 978-0-595-43118-2 (pbk)
ISBN: 978-0-595-87461-3 (ebk)

Printed in the United States of America

To

Lou Lovelace
For her loving interest in putting my words into readable style.

My Husband Henry M. Bachmann
For Love and support on all levels

My Dad Olin K. Smith
For putting the final book together

Dr. Paul Leon Masters
For believing I have what it takes to write books

Contents

Author's Personal Message

Starting at a very young age, especially in my early teens, I discovered that I naturally had an intense yearning to know Who God really was on a personally intimate level, and to also know who I was as one who is 'in fact!' made in the perfect image and likeness of God. I am happy to say that this most incredible and inspiring of life-expanding journey for me is still in *process*, and I imagine and hope that it always will be! I can honestly say that every day of my life is, and has been, a most amazing adventure filled with life-transforming questions and answers as to *how to* live life in a more spiritually advantageous manner.

For this reason I sincerely desire to convey to you, communicated through the written word from my heart and soul, the same excitement that I have experienced throughout the years about attaining my own inner experience and realization of oneness with the Presence of God! I desire to share with you the experience of personally knowing the living, and very real Presence of God, Who always resides within our own innermost beingness. And by so doing, experience a personal relationship with yourself in which you find yourself to be one of the most exceptional persons you have ever had the good fortune to meet!

This wonderful search for self-knowledge has also led me to discover that I am, and you are, a remarkably multitalented expression of the divine nature of God. You and I are the unique expressions through which the unconditionally loving Presence of God expresses. I came to experience, through daily meditational practices and daily spiritual study, that I already was *one with* the truth that I had been searching to know and discover. This search for self-understanding and personal growth, combined with living a daily existence filled with the glorious Presence of God, has brought to me, throughout the years, specific *spiritualized lessons* and how to methods for self-improvement and spiritual transformation. Many of these exceptionally self-transforming lessons and *how to* methods for living a better life are described in this book. The knowledge that I have gained about myself, and my relationship with God, from working with these lessons, has literally saved my life—emotionally, mentally, physically, and spiritually! It is for this reason that I desire, *from a sincere heart*, to share these lessons with you, as I have wholeheartedly shared and lovingly desired to help many others throughout the past years of ministerial teaching and counseling.

My greatest joy and devotion in this life is to know the Presence of God within myself to a greater degree and with a finer clarity of understanding than ever before, each and every day. My next greatest joy is to know my true God-Self to a greater degree today than I did yesterday. I strive to accomplish this learning every day by heeding the d*ivine teachings* of the Presence of God revealed to me through my heartfelt desire to listen firsthand to the *still inner voice* of God. In addition, my primary joy is to share with you the answers that I have found from my own life of struggle, suffering, pain, and search for freedom, of how to live the triumphant life that God created us to live!

Personally, my principal goal in this life has been to overcome all fear by knowing that—

- In my oneness with the Presence and healing truth of God, there is no lack or limitation!

This greatest of all spiritual truths has been the *divinely-revealed foundational truth upon which my teachings are based*. For many years I have found it to be a remarkably *exhilarating and growth-producing challenge* to personally strive to demonstrate this marvelous truth in my own life. Furthermore, I am happy to say that I am still excited by the daily challenge that come my way through which I am granted the divine opportunities to learn, to an even greater degree, this most self-liberating of spiritual truths!

Even though I have used these lessons for many years for my own healing and transformation of my daily life and I have successfully used these teachings to share healing and personal transformation with those that have come to me for teaching, counseling, healing, and sharing—I still use these teachings today for my own continually expanded healing and personal transformation. And I can assure you that I intend to continue to work with these lessons for added spiritualized-personal development and expansion throughout my entire life.

For example—A couple of days ago, I worked with Lesson One, "Transforming Your Personality Through the Tool of Meditation." As I worked with the meditative exercise for "Spiritual Transformation" contained within Lesson One, I experienced the following revelation: I became still within a contemplative state and I asked myself—

- If I were spiritually illumined right now, if I knew without a shadow of a doubt that I was made in the perfect image and likeness of God, what divine quality would I be excited about expressing?

As I listened to my heart-center I was filled with the feeling of having and experiencing complete *freedom*. A freedom which is based on the spiritual principle which affirms that—

- God is the one and only power. The one and only power of God is the manifestation-power, which creates only abundant good from the Consciousness of God, Who is only aware of unlimited and All-present goodness.

As I worked with the next step of contemplating how I would *personally feel* if I knew without any doubt that God is the one and only power acting within me and in my life—I felt, experienced, and really knew a greater state of freedom then I have ever realized before. I then understood and experienced within myself that I have the complete freedom to be perfect and to live a spiritually-perfect life because God is the only power acting in and through me and my life. I thoroughly comprehended that God is the only power acting in my life, and that there is no other power that can stand in the way of my own perfection, or stand in the way of my life being the outer manifestation and expression of God's exact law of perfection and harmony! I now know that I am completely free to be the spiritually-perfect person I was created to be and to live the spiritually-perfect life that God created for me to live. This experience was one of the greatest experiences of *real unencumbered freedom* that I have ever felt up to this point. I experienced the spiritual reality of what it is like to live a life that is completely free from all lack and limitation because God is the one and only power! This experience was, and still is, incredibly fantastic and personally liberating!

As I preceded to work with the next step in this exercise: I rested in my oneness with the Presence of God and I asked to be filled with, to personally experience, God's revelation of what true spiritualized freedom, based on *God as the one and only power expressing through me and through my life*—felt like. As I did this, I was blessed with a divine vision. Within this divinely-revealed vision, I saw my human, personal body lying flat on the floor, and from my heart-center, slowly resurrected the living form of Christ with his arms outstretched and reaching for heaven.

I then proceeded to intuitively discern the symbolism of this vision, which God had revealed to me. My prone body represented my false, human, personal self, which still felt (to some degree) separated from the full power of God expressing through my personal self and through my personal life experience. This false, human, personal self soon ceased to exist as the truth of the Christ, the living expression of the All-power of God, resurrected and rose forth from my heart-center of unconditional love. I then perceived that I was made anew in the image and likeness of God. I then knew that I was the living offspring (the living expression) of God. I understood that the All-power of God's Presence was fully expressing through me. I now comprehend that my true God-Self is the living, perfect instrument through which the All-power of God's goodness is being made manifest within me and throughout my daily life experience!

As I continued with the final part of this extraordinary meditative exercise, I not only knew that the day before me would be filled with the freedom to feel empowered by God, but that my entire life throughout eternity would never be filled with any real or lasting sense of fear, limitation, or restriction—ever again!

As you can very well understand, I was ecstatically grateful that I had taken just twenty minutes out of my busy morning to work with a meditative exercise which I had previously worked with for years!

Further example—Several weeks ago I was intuitively led to work with Lesson Ten, "Living the Life that You Desire." I reread the particularly instructive and transformative lesson contained within *Day Two*, which is described as follows:

• When you meditate, let go of your personal will so that your mind and heart are filled with the thoughts, will, and the desires of God. Let go completely of any sense of your personal, limited will being done, a personal will that may be filled with a false sense of discontent about your life. Let the divine desire, the divine Will of God fill you with feelings of happiness and contented satisfaction throughout the whole day.

As I meditated upon this truth I literally experienced the Presence of God within myself desiring to express *through me* the life-expanding emotional energy of enthusiasm; a God-ordained, God-inspired, and God-directed enthusiasm about bringing into physical evidence the grandeur of God's creative magnificence and power to create unlimited fulfillment in my life. Needless to say, I was literally in *seventh heaven* throughout the entire day and I know that I will be throughout my life.

Just through my intent and desire to take twenty minutes to meditate in the morning, I became intimately aware of how often we hold back the true brilliance of God's Presence expressing through us by being in a personally less than positive emotional state. I experienced just how important it is for all of us to let go of any negative or restrictive emotional state that we may be in so that the truth of

God's magnificent Self-reality can be known through us, as us, each and every day! I realized that this is the way that we are meant to live our lives each and every day! Through this meditative practice, I realized that all of us are the literal creation of the perfect image that God has had of each of us throughout eternity, and that it is time for us to live the reality of that divinely-perfect image once and for all, right here and now!

The meditative exercise that I just described to you was even more fascinating to me because I have worked with this specific meditative exercise for a good thirty years. And it still amazes me how incredibly phenomenal it is to realize and experience a new aspect of God's living Presence within myself. It also reminds me that the living Presence of God is truly infinite, thus the knowingness and realization of God's Presence is an infinitely-expansive process for us all.

Each of the lessons contained within this book has been the result of entering into daily states of meditation and allowing the inspiration and divine guidance of God to be revealed. I have lovingly, sincerely, and genuinely dedicated the majority of my daily life (from my early teenage years onward) to entering into union with the Presence of God within my mind and heart and seeking God's divine guidance as to how to live a spiritually-perfect and Truth-filled life. Each lesson has been personally revealed to me, within quiet *contemplative* meditation and *listening* heart-centered prayer, from the Heart and Mind of God's Presence as to the necessary steps to take for personal growth and transformation. The personal lessons recorded within this book have helped me throughout the years and I am enthusiastically honored to share them with you!

Since my early teens I not only have had a natural desire to know God and myself completely, but I have also had an unwavering passion throughout the years to study various religious teachings and spiritually-oriented philosophical thought systems. My main emphasis of study has been on the Judeo-Christian philosophy, Christianity (the true teachings of Christ), Hinduism, Buddhism, and mysticism (personal union with God). My personal research, study, and love of these spiritual teachings has led me to be *earnestly collective* in my approach for God-knowledge and self-knowledge versus being a settled and dedicated expert in only one specific religious study. It is from innumerable spiritual principles, originating from most of the major religious thought systems, which constitute the intellectual background and foundation from which my study courses and personal teachings are founded.

Throughout the years I have been divinely led to study many of the universally-known spiritual principles of this world's religious teachings by the genuine yearning of my heart. My heart has also led me to rely on and seek the divine guidance, inspiration, revelation, and teachings of the living Presence of God, Who resides within my heart-center. I have been led by my earnest heart and pure soul nature to blend these two forms of knowledge and soul-searching together for the acquisition of the highest of universally-divine teachings. It is this personalized teaching that I now sincerely, honestly, and genuinely share with you. May your journey along the spiritual path be filled with the absolute reality of God's unconditional love, health, and wholeness. And may you also have a spirit of joyfulness, delight, excitement, and unlimited fun as you do so!

Introduction

Within each of us is an inner divine self, our True-God-Self, who longs to be free of the imprisonment and bondage of our own limited beliefs about God, about ourselves, about our lives, and about others. These limited and false beliefs are the outgrowth of a world that is ignorant of its own spiritual heritage.

Throughout this book, the tools of daily spiritual study and the actual putting into practice of specific spiritual practices will be used as a vehicle to help strip away the layers of limited thought and belief from our human psyche, so that we will be free to be the Spiritually Perfect Being that we are all created to be. At the center of ourselves we find a divine Self who is naturally loving, virtuous, and perfect. It is this true, divine Self that we seek to uncover through the daily practices that are contained within this book of study-course lessons. Each lesson is specifically geared towards experiencing a literal and intimate knowledge of God. Through the daily experience of *attaining oneness* with the Presence of God, you will also come to see, realize, and know the reality of who *you are* as made in the perfect image and likeness of God. Only by knowing who you really are through the art of meditation and daily spiritual practices—can you be who you are really meant to be in this life. The beautiful journey that takes you within yourself brings you face to face with your true Self, a divine Self, who is the perfect incarnation of God's Presence expressed within the beauty of your individual and unique Self. Learning to live this grand, divine manifestation of the personal spiritual expression of God that you are, is the only way to achieve the freedom that you desire from all of the hurts, pain, and insecurities of this world. *How wonderful it is to awaken one day and look at yourself and there you see, feel, and know that you are the living expression of all of the perfection that you have ever yearned to be!*

These study-course lessons will address the need for daily spiritual disciplines and practices that are used for the attainment of spiritual enlightenment in our everyday western world.

- We will study and use spiritual disciplines and practices that help to clear the mind of the false-limited-ego self so that the God-Self can take over—which will result in the greater living of health, love, happiness, security, and an experience of over-all fulfillment in this world.

- We will study the steps and *how to* methods used to integrate these spiritual practices and disciplines into our western mind-set. Through daily work with these lessons, we will seek to find a higher maturity of self. We will find a way that we can grow from the pain, which is felt within the interior of our everyday thoughts and emotions, to a higher level of spiritual reality, which will lead us to a real and lasting sense of internal freedom. With daily practice we will elevate the internal belief system that we hold of ourselves. We will bring about needed changes within ourselves by achieving union with the living Presence of God that resides within our own minds and hearts.

As each of us desires to pursue the path of personalized spiritual growth and enlightenment, we do this so that we may experience growth within our own personal perception of our life and ourselves. If we do not take the time to put the importance of our personalized spiritual growth first in our daily lives, then we will be unable to handle the problems, hurts, and pains that we face today any better than we have in the past. As we seek the understanding of God, the understanding of spiritual principle, and the understanding of ourselves, we gain insight into the process of attaining real and provable spiritual enlightenment within ourselves. We begin to experience for ourselves the reality of the attainment of the goals of spiritual truth being demonstrated in our daily lives and realize that our lives are abundantly worthwhile and sacred. We begin to experience the process of fulfillment in our personal lives which brings to us a greater sense of personal health, better relationships, and a life that is far better today than the life that we were living yesterday.

The use of the intellect through the process of daily study and learning of spiritual truth is the first step towards gaining a personal awareness of your true divinity. When you intellectually know that you really are made in the perfect image and likeness of God, you will start to notice an inner change in the way that you think about yourself, your life, and others that are in your life. When you find your inner perception of life changing for the better, you will also find that the outer events of your life will also change for the better. As you enthusiastically look forward to using your *daily spiritual practices* to change your inner perception about life, you will find your outer life activities taking on greater meaning and experience a feeling of aliveness and more vitality than ever before.

There are numerous religions and teachings that are based on positive thinking and spiritual principles that originate from a wide variety of spiritual truths that are beneficial and necessary—but many are lacking in presenting a workable system of study which includes the necessary ingredients for spiritual growth. These necessary and transforming steps consist of the daily study of spiritual principles, the daily practice of meditation (union with the Presence of God), and daily spiritual practices. The religious teachings of the world tend to fail to address the *how to methods* of overcoming the negative aspects within the psyche of the personality, which hides the pure spiritual God-Self from view. Within this book you will find practical, easy, non-denominational or inter-denominational, spiritually reliable *how to methods* for the western mind to heal the negative aspects of the psyche so that the Presence of God can be personally known.

Within the study-methods that I have intuitively developed throughout many years of personal devotion, self-study, and the desire to live a more enriching and less painful life—I hope to encourage each one of you to solve your own personal problems—by taking personal responsibility for the state of your own life experience. As we each realize that we are responsible for our perception, and oftentimes the creation of our life experience, then we are ready to work with the spiritual truths that will help us re-create the lives we desire to live—through working with the *how to methods* which show the way to change the beliefs of the conscious and subconscious states of mind, so that change for the positive is possible.

The daily *how to* methods that I present in this book do require daily practice, dedication, and enthusiastic participation. These lessons are an exciting challenge towards the expansion of consciousness, which creates an outer expansion of positive experience. The great truth is that each individual can change their reality. We change our personal reality by the examination of our thoughts and feelings, and then changing these thoughts and feelings so that we are reflecting the positive qualities that we desire. This change can only come about through daily union with the living and real Presence of God within your heart and mind, through daily introspection of yourself, by the practice of a daily regimen of principle and study, along with workable how to methods and practices that will guide you to the changes that you need to make within yourself. As you practice and work with these lessons daily—lessons, which are based on the study of principle, meditation, visualization, affirmation, and daily how to steps to follow in your everyday experience—you learn to use the whole extent of your creative mind in cooperation or union with the essential and precious qualities of your soul.

The conscious mind is used for the intellectual and reasoning properties for study. The subconscious mind is worked with and changed through the tools of reason, meditation, visualization, and affirmations for the integration of truth into the deeper recesses of the mind. The superconscious soul-mind reveals the need for daily contact with God, which is necessary for any real and lasting change to take place.

Through personal study I have found a practical, transformative, and workable teaching system that includes the necessary ingredients that will help guide the sincere and serious student of spirituality to acquire immense growth within themselves and within their lives.

The time and attention that you place on becoming spiritually whole is the most important time that you can ever spend in this lifetime. Make a commitment from this day forward to being God in expression—to truly be the "Light of the world." Come out from under the limited false beliefs that you hold of yourself and be one with the grandeur that God created you to be. Welcome to the adventure of knowing and living the greatest life experience that you have ever known—which is a life that is filled with abundant love, health, happiness, fulfillment, and divine purpose!

Each Soul that incarnates into this world is the Divine representation of the all-inclusive Light of God.

Within each Soul is the blueprint for the successful living of that Soul's Divine Purpose, here on earth at this time.

Through the vehicle of daily spiritual study, practice, and the use of various spiritual disciplines, each one is then equipped to bring forth that one's full expression of the presence of Divinity that resides within them.

Stand-up and declare with a loud voice—that you are the Light of the world, that is here, to be **One** *with God in the internal and external world around you.*

Today is rich with the blessings of God—rejoice and live forever in the internal and eternal splendor of your special and unique spiritual magnificence!"

1

Transforming Your Personality Through The Tool Of Meditation

The Art of Meditation and Your Tie to Yourself

Author's note: The following lesson has been personally worked with and divinely interpreted from the truth of the teachings of Christ, which reveal the following realities of our Divine Selfhood.

Each of us is made in the perfect image and likeness of God.

Each of us is to show forth the divine qualities and attributes of God within our-selves through the example of our everyday lives.

Each of us becomes the perfection of God through the renewing and recreating of our mind (thinking process) and nature (emotional psyche.)

There are many reasons to meditate and there are various techniques of meditation available to the public today. This lesson will look at a tech-nique of meditation that will be used as a tool to answer the question of how to attain a personal relationship and reality with the Presence of God. This personal relationship and reality that you create with God will, in turn, lead you to the answer of who you are within your oneness with the Pres-ence of God. Within the experience of your realized unity and oneness with God, you will also be led on the inspiring inner journey of attaining true knowledge and universal wisdom.

Many in the world today ask the same universal questions that our ancestors sought. We all seek the internal knowledge that will reveal to us the origin of who we are. Sit for a moment, look within yourself, and ask yourself the following questions:

1. *Do you know the Real you*

2. *Do you really Love and Honor yourself?*

3. *Do you have a sense of Real and Lasting self-confidence?*

The answers to these questions are what we all seek to know. Meditation is the fastest and easiest way to know yourself, to love yourself, and to be self-confident. Whenever you meditate, you come face to face with yourself; you come face to face with your personal human self; and, you come face to face with your true spiritual Self.

- When you meditate you are able to become still enough so that you can have a close look at who you really are. In this time of inner introspection you can view the parts of your personality that are less than what you really want to be, that are less than how you would like to act, and the parts of yourself that feel less than the wonderful feelings that you would like to feel.

- When you meditate you also come to view and become acquainted with the true spiritual Self that you are when all of the pretenses of this world are gone from your mind and thought processes.

In the outer world of daily experience, we come face to face with the same two parts of ourselves—our spiritually perfect Self and our less than perfect human self. For example: You may find yourself in an argument with a loved one where you feel that you cannot really express the truth that you want to, in order that harmony and truth are present in your relationship. So you find yourself at odds with the inner self of yourself that seems to be less than clear, strong, and self-confident. But you know that there is also a spiritually strong, loving, and wise part of yourself that can also be expressed within that relationship. So you work on yourself and practice in many relationships until you overcome the pain of self-limitation, and you start to live the true Self that you want to live in your daily life.

You can do the same work on yourself using meditation—which is a much less painful way to see the true spiritual Self that you are. You are then able to work with this true Self to bring about rightful change, and then you are able to express your spiritually whole and balanced Self in your outside world of experience and relationships.

You Cannot Run Away from Yourself—

In everyday life and experience you can run away from yourself for quite awhile but you never live the life that you desire to live. With meditation you no longer want to run away from yourself, for the Self that you come to know within the practice of meditation fills you with a real sense of peace and pleasure that far out-weighs any of the growing pains that you may encounter.

Running away from yourself, running away from learning about yourself, is one of the most harmful traits that block you from your spiritual growth. Yet most people today are doing just that, they are running away from themselves as far and as fast as they can and then, they are left with nothing.

> *Within the following analysis, we will look at several typical ways that people run away from seeing and knowing the spiritual truth of who they are through knowledge of ourselves, we find inner illuminating and personal healing.*

Through Activity—

When you are constantly busy you will not have the time to study and observe yourself. Most people today are so busy that they run all day long and then fall into exhausted sleep at the end of the day without a thought of God or of their spiritual growth. How sad it is to be so busy that one lives out this life without knowing what this life is all about!

- Make time for yourself. Put the time that you meditate and study about your spiritual life—first. Your spiritual growth must be your first priority in this life. When you put your spiritual life first, your everyday life will become much more valuable to you. When you start out your day by joining with the divine wisdom of God's Presence, *which resides within your mind and heart*, you will find that you are intuitively aware of a greater wisdom than you yourself have humanly available to you. This greater divine wisdom is always guiding you as to the spiritually-honest words to say, the spiritually-appropriate emotions to feel, the spiritually-rational thoughts to think, and the correct action and decisions to make in your life. In proportion to your commitment to working with yourself spiritually, each and everyday, you will find that within every negative emotion that you experience—you will be intuitively aware that there is an opposite divinely-superior, positive emotion which you are being guided to express instead. In the same way, you will find that within every negative thought that you think—you will be intuitively aware that there is an opposite divinely-dependable, truth-filled, trustworthy, positive thought which you are being guided to focus on instead.

Denial—

When we deny that there is any area within our emotional and spiritual psyche where we can grow further, then we are in a state of spiritual and emotional denial that brings about a state of stagnation. When people say that they are spiritually perfect and yet most of their life is miserable, then there is a problem.

• Be sure to always be in a state of teach-ability. Within the practice of daily meditation, the true student *who has been meditating for many, many years* will know that each meditation brings to them some new insight about themselves and about God. I know that every time that I meditate something exciting happens to me. I know that I will never be completely satisfied with my current level of spiritual growth and understanding. I will always want to know and learn more about my life and myself. I will continually want to understand, to a greater degree, the internal workings of the human and divine psyches of others. And most important of all, to learn more about the All-Knowing universal Psyche of God's Presence, which always resides within the innermost center of my beingness, Who is also the source of my true God-Self-Reality!

Love Relationships—

Many people run away from themselves by constantly being in a love relationship that is having problems, or always being in a state of misery because they do not have someone to love. Relationships that are not going right, or where one is looking for Mr. or Ms. Right, is a great waste of your time and emotional energy.

• When you take the time to meditate and know the truth of yourself and of God, your love relationships will be much more harmonious. You will intuitively know how to heal any of the emotions and thoughts of separation that may try to take from you and your relationships in this life, the true spiritually-healing substance of unconditional, unrestricted, divine love. Within your meditative ability to rest in and be filled with God's unconditional love, you will find yourself becoming free from the belief in any outer false forces of lack and limitation that can take your God-given sense of wholeness and completeness from you. Thus, you will be a whole and complete person within yourself who will always be in an inner state of purity and harmlessness. Therefore, you will be a person from whom the unconditional love of God will: always be in operation and action; always be available; and always be a mighty influence to heal all that is unlike divinely-unconditional love, within yourself, within others, and within the energy and life of your relationships. When you know who you are, when you truly know that you are indeed whole and complete within yourself—through the daily use of introspective mystical meditation—then, and only then, will you draw to yourself other individuals who are spiritually perfect for you.

Excitement—

Constantly looking for outside excitement is a classic way of running away from whom you are. Much of this world is made up of the escapism's that bring one into the energy of excitability. The misdirected focus of excitement can waste your health, your soul, and your life. The endless search for excitement in the outer world can lead one to the complete loss of who they really are.

• True excitement comes when you are peaceful and sure within yourself. Excitement comes when you realize a spiritual secret of the universe in meditation, or when you feel the Presence of God within you every moment of the day—now this is a reason to be really excited!

Resentment-Anger-Hurt-Criticism—

All of these negative emotions keep you locked within the state of victim-hood and self-pity that leads nowhere. Each of these negative feelings keeps you intertwined within the framework of negativity that draws a veil between where you are and where you want to be. By having the ability to see above the negative picture, you are led to a true state of spiritual freedom.

• Daily meditation works through the layers of negative emotions until you achieve a state of inner clarity that frees you from the hurt that these negative emotions create.

Non-Commitment—

Being in a continual state of non-commitment stems from the inner belief that you lack the self-confidence that is necessary to follow through on any commitment that you make in your life.

- When you face yourself in daily meditation, you know that you have all that it takes to be successful in whatever undertaking you choose.

Problems and Dramas—

Problems and dramas keep your attention focused on the outer picture of this life, much in the same way that one can waste the whole day by looking at one soap opera after another on the television set.

- In meditation you naturally work through any problems or dramas that may come up in your life so that you have the freedom to live the spiritually-fulfilled life that you desire to live.

    Whenever you run away from facing, understanding, healing, any of the problems that you may face in your everyday life experience, you are literally running away from yourself.

In meditation you make a commitment to yourself to face yourself totally—you can then stop running away from yourself, at least for a short period of time. At some point in your daily meditations, you will find it easier and easier to be with yourself. You will slowly learn to really love the self that you see. You can then stop running away altogether and start to live. You can start to be the person that you really want to be—which is loving, strong, dependable, trustworthy, and fearless—within yourself and within your interactions with others.

When you face your inner fears through the art of meditation, you will gain the most wonderful freedom that you have ever experienced. You will start to really love the 'You' with which you come face to face. When you can really love yourself, then you can really love others.

When you are afraid to know yourself, other people sense this and they are uneasy around you. *Fear shows itself in the inner feelings of uncertainty, lack of self-confidence, not being able to make commitments, being undependable and selfish.* Remember, that what you do to other people, you are really doing to yourself. You are not facing yourself because of the lack of love that you feel towards yourself.

In meditation you learn to know who you are. In meditation you can work with whatever needs changing within your personality and learn to love your real God-Self-Reality that is hidden deep within yourself.

- Within the following transformational meditative techniques you will learn to: *Make a personal connection between your personality and the perfect personality and Presence of God.* The false human sense of who you are, *your human personality*, is generally based upon the false beliefs and teachings of this world. The false beliefs of this world define who you are as one who is imperfect, because the false beliefs of this world mistakenly believe that you are somehow separated from the perfection of the Presence of God living in you and through you. Through the tool of meditation you will rediscover your true spiritually-perfect personality. This true, spiritualized personality is based on the spiritual truth of your eternal oneness with the presence, the power, the unconditional love, and the perfection of the Presence of God that is now, always has been, and forever will be within the conscious awareness of your mind and heart.

- *Learn to use meditation for the strengthening of this union with the Presence of God within your heart.* Through the daily use of the tool of meditation, you will learn to turn away from the stresses and falsities of this world, to enter into the quiet and calm inner reality of who you really are, as one who is made in the perfect image and likeness of God, and as one who is fully and freely expressing the divine qualities and attributes of the perfection of God's divine nature.

- *Learn the practice of knowing the Life and Presence of God.* By means of following the daily practice of meditation, you will become intimately knowledgeable about the true Presence of God that resides within your mind, *the seat of your conscious awareness,* and within the true feeling nature of your heart, *wherein resides the pure and unrestricted expressions of positiveness.*

- Learn to use the strength within yourself and focus this strength for the higher use of your true God-Self in your daily self-expression.

MEDITATION EXERCISE NUMBER ONE
SPIRITUAL TRANSFORMATION

With this meditative technique, you will come to realize the spiritual truth that is within yourself. You will touch the reality of God and make the spiritual truth of God a part of who you are. Within this miraculous meditative exercise you will be using your intellect or mind to decide which divine qualities or attributes you desire to be and express at this time. Then you will be joining with the reality

*of the specific divine quality or attribute within your heart, or feeling and emo-
tional center; then you will experience the mystical reality of the Presence of God
revealing to you the divine quality or attribute with which you are working, as
God knows it to be. Work with the following meditation exercise for ten to
twenty minutes, once or twice a day, for a week, month, or for whatever length of
time it takes for you to fully accept and become the divine quality with which you
are working.*

First—Become still, and within a contemplative state ask yourself—If I were
spiritually illumined right now, if I knew without a shadow of a doubt that I was
made in the perfect image and likeness of God right now, what divine qualities,
what divine attributes would I be excited about expressing?

In a notebook, write down the divine qualities and attributes that have just
spoken to you from your soul. Now go over the list and pick a divine quality or
attribute that you would like to work on becoming, at this time. Pick a divine
quality or attribute that will create a level of great interest within yourself, that
will hold your attention. Work with your chosen divine quality until it becomes a
fully-integrated part of your personality; then work with another divine quality or
attribute on your list that attracts your attention. Periodically renew your list of
divine attributes and divine qualities that you desire to *become one with* and
express.

STEPS FOR CONNECTING WITH THE DIVINE ATTRIBUTES OF GOD

Step One—Relaxation

- Close your eyes and relax your body, mind, and emotions completely. Your
  purpose is to relax yourself so that you are comfortable and then you can forget your body, mind, and emotions. Your intent and purpose is to be inwardly
  calm and mentally alert. Any position that is comfortable is fine. I find it easier
  to relax if I do a few simple yoga exercises before I meditate.

Step Two—Focus Your Mind and Heart

For five to ten minutes focus your mind and heart on the emotional reality of your chosen divine attribute or quality—express that choice and become one with it.

- **Being Fearless**—work on the feeling of being without fear. Ask yourself—How would you feel without the feeling of fear? How would you feel if you knew that you were truly and absolutely dauntless, daring, and brave? How would you live your daily life without the limiting and restrictive inner feeling of fearful apprehension; to be completely worry-free and self-assured about your ability to handle life in an appropriate way? What decisions would you make if you were completely courageous? How would you express the truth of who you are to others if you fearlessly knew that *you were whole, complete, and perfect within yourself?*

- **With absolute self-confidence**—work on the feeling of having absolute self-confidence. Ask yourself—How would you feel if you were completely self-confident? What decisions would you make in your life, right now, if you knew you could do anything? How would you interact with others that are in your life if you were completely sure of yourself?

- **Feeling fully alive**—work on the feeling of being fully alive! Ask yourself—How would you feel if you just could not wait to express your joy for being fully and completely alive to the world around you this day? How would you act if you were completely free to express your joy for being fully alive during the day, free from any self-imposed internal restrictions that stand in the way of your expressing and feeling your lively exuberance? What would your energy level feel like if you allowed yourself to be and express aliveness fully and completely?

- **Being happy**—work on feeling really happy. Ask yourself—If you were really happy with yourself, how would you feel about yourself whenever you thought about yourself during the day? If you were happy and contented about yourself and your life, how would you act during the day when alone and/or in the company of others? If you were happy within yourself, what decisions would you make about your life? What friends would you choose to be around if your number one priority was to be cheerful the majority of the time? How would your body feel if you were filled with the feelings of delight, content-ment, and true inner happiness with yourself, with others, and with your life?

Be sure to pick subjects and traits that you are sincerely interested in developing within yourself. Concentrate on the theme of your subject and let each thought lead you to the next, until you feel at one with the quality, which you are working with developing.

Step Three—Oneness with God

For five to ten minutes rest in your oneness with God; feel that you and the divine nature of God are one within the energy, within the reality, within the vibrational field of the quality with which you are working. Join with the Heart of God, the pure feeling nature of God's Presence within yourself, and ask God to reveal to you, to fill you with, to express through you, to *feel* the divine quality that you are working with, through your *receptive* feeling nature. Let God fill you with the spiritual reality of the trait with which you are working.

- **Being fearless**—as you rest within your oneness with the reality of the energy of being fearless, the intuitive guidance of God fills you with an inner sureness that knows, without a shadow of a doubt, that God *is the one and only power* in your life; therefore, you now *fully realize* that there is *no other power* to cause you to ever feel afraid again! You totally feel, and are immersed in, the All-power of God flowing throughout your entire body, mind, and emotional nature. You find yourself becoming fully aware that God's Presence, which is now being revealed to you as the One and only Power, is with you continually throughout every day and every night, throughout eternity.

- **Absolute Self-Confidence**—as you rest within your oneness with the reality of the energy of having absolute self-confidence, the intuitive guidance of God fills you with an internal image of yourself as one who is completely self-confi-dent. Within this image you have an inner surety, an inner knowingness that this spiritually-intuitive emotional reality of self-confidence is 'now' the truth of who you are. Together with this divine image of your self-confident Self, you may also see an image of yourself that is doing a specific line of work that you were never, up to this point, aware that you had the ability to do. Perhaps you now feel that this image of yourself, accomplishing this specific and special work, is your life's purpose.

- **Feeling Fully Alive**—as you rest within your oneness with the reality of the energy of feeling fully alive, the intuitive guidance of God fills you with an internal emotional reality of one who is completely filled with the essence, the reality of knowing that your life is indeed eternal! You find that you intuitively perceive that the life that you are now living is the eternal life of God living through you! Now you are alive with the feeling and knowledge that knows that your very life is sacred and extremely special!

- **Being Happy**—as you rest within your oneness with the reality of, the energy of, being happy, the intuitive guidance of God fills you with an overwhelming feeling of bliss, ecstasy, and exhilaration for no reason at all—meaning that the great happiness that you are now feeling is not dependent on anyone or anything outside of yourself. You find that you are now being filled with the Presence of God, which is realized as bliss, happiness, and ecstasy, and now you know that the realized Presence of God is all that you will ever need to be in a continual state of happiness!

Remember that the divine guidance of God, revealed to us as our own special truth, can come to us in many and various ways of expression. God may speak to us through a thought, through a feeling, through an image, through a vision, or through a symbol. Be aware that the diverse voice of God is always positive, unconditionally loving, and enhanced with a liberal amount of free will.

Step Four—Slowly Return

Slowly return to the world around you and put into action the reality of the divine quality which you have just been experiencing Now, work on using the insight that you have just achieved, within your mediation period, in the midst of your outer activities during the day. Actually and actively put the reality and authenticity of the—realization of your oneness with the divine quality with which you have just worked—into concrete action

- **Being Fearless**—take the inner reality that you have just experienced in meditation of what being fearless feels like, from your meditative experience with steps two and three of this exercise, and feel that sense of fearlessness throughout the whole day.

- On a personal level, through your meditative work with step two, you will firmly commit yourself to feeling and being free from apprehension and worry about your ability to handle any problem that comes your way, no matter what, throughout the day. You will know that *in your oneness with the Divine, All-Knowing wisdom of God* that you will be filled with the appropriate answers to every problem that you may encounter throughout the day.

- On a divinely intuitive level, through your meditative work with step three, you will negate, sublimate, transcend, and heal every feeling of fear by declaring, knowing, and affirming that God is the One and only Power working in your life.

- **With Absolute Self Confidence**—take the inner reality that you just experienced in meditation of what having absolute self-confidence feels like from your meditative experience with steps two and three of this exercise, and feel that sense of absolute self-confidence throughout the whole day.

- On a personal level, through your meditative work with step two, you will commit yourself to feeling and being self-confident throughout the day, by greeting everyone that you meet from an inner state of openness and friendliness, regardless of who they are and how they respond to you.

- On a divinely intuitive level, through your meditative work with step three, you now know, from the divine vision that you had of yourself doing a special kind of work, which fills you with excitement, that there are definite daily steps for you to take to bring your divine purpose into actuality. Each day you now find yourself being guided to the daily steps that are necessary for you to be able to *put into action* the divinely special work that you now feel guided to accept and achieve for yourself.

- **Feeling Fully Alive**—take the inner reality that you just experienced in meditation of what feeling fully alive feels like, *from your meditative experience with steps two and three of this exercise*, and feel that sense of aliveness throughout the whole day.

- On a personal level, *through your meditative work with step two*, you will consciously commit yourself to feeling an unrestricted energy level of feeling fully alive throughout the day, because you are now allowing yourself to fully and freely feel joy for yourself and for your life.

- On a divinely intuitive level, *through your meditative work with step three*, you will now know, throughout the whole day, that you and your life are divinely sacred and special, regardless of any feelings that may try to tell you that you are ordinary and/or that your life is just the same old routine.

- **Being Happy**—take the inner reality that you just experienced in meditation of what true happiness feels like, *from your meditative experience with steps two and three of this exercise,* and feel that sense of happiness throughout the whole day.

- On a personal level, *through your meditative work with step two,* you will now commit yourself to feeling happy throughout the day, whenever you find yourself being overly critical about yourself. You will now commit yourself to being happy about yourself, *because you are made in the perfect image and likeness of God,* every time you feel the temptation to put yourself down.

- On a divinely intuitive level, *through your meditative work with step three,* you will gladly know, throughout the whole day, that you and the Presence of God, *experienced as bliss, ecstasy, and happiness,* is with you all of the time!

- Follow this format with whatever divine attribute, quality, or ideal you are working with during the time of your meditation period.

MEDITATION EXERCISE NUMBER TWO CONTEMPLATIVE 7-DAY UNION WITH THE IDEAL PERSONALITY OF GOD

Take each ideal of the personality of God, one per day from the list that follows, which make-up, in part, the true personality of God and filter the personality of God into your conscious awareness. Do the following exercise for a week, month, or for however long you feel intuitively guided to do so.

Day One

- I am the unconditional love of God in expression

Day Two

- I live each day as a creative divine adventure!

Day Three

- I am the positiveness of God's personality in daily expression.

Day Four

- I live each day—fully alive with divine enthusiasm!

Day Five

- I am the peace of God that heals all disharmony in my life.

Day Six

- My true God-Self-Reality is bound to the personality of God and I reflect All that God is.

Day Seven

- I am filled with the inner strength of God—so that I can do and be All that I am spiritually.

STEPS FOR ACHIEVING UNION WITH THE PERSONALITY OF GOD

Step One—Relaxation

- Close your eyes and relax your body, mind, and emotions completely. When you have achieved an inner sense of relaxation—join with the Presence of God that is within your mind and heart. The Presence of God will be felt as an inner sense of peace, unconditional love, and excitement for the high attainment of the divine ideal of the personality of God with which you are about to become united. Your intent and purpose is to be calm and mentally alert to the reality of the divine ideal of the personality of God expressing through you. Your intent is to be one in nature with the divine ideal of the personality of God that you are contemplating—and on which you are fully focused.

Step Two—Focus Your Mind and Heart

- For five to ten minutes focus your mind on the emotional reality of the divine ideal of God's personality which is specified for the day (from the above list): Keep your attention, mentally and emotionally, centered on the divine ideal of the personality of God that you desire *to become one with* and express. Focus on the ideal of God's personality (that you are to work with specifically during the day) and let yourself become The Divine ideal on which you are concentrating.

- For example—on the first day as you are working on the divine ideal, *I am the unconditional love of God,* you slowly and calmly repeat this truth silently to yourself (repeatedly) until you feel yourself peacefully becoming—one with the inner reality of this truth.

- At this point, you then connect with the inner intuitive feeling nature of this truth by asking yourself the following questions: *How do I feel within myself inasmuch as I know that I am the unconditional love of God in expression? Knowing and feeling that I am truly the unconditional love of God in expression—how will I interact with every person that comes into my day? How do I now feel about myself, as one who is always worthy of being loved unconditionally by God?*

- Ask yourself: How would you feel and live if you were already *one with* the divine quality of God with which you are working and becoming consciously aware? Allow yourself to be the energy of, the reality of, and the divine truth of God expressing through you. Remember that you are working on fully realizing the divine truth or personal divine reality of who you already are, deep within the consciousness of your soul or spirit.

Step Three—Oneness with God

- For five to ten minutes—rest in your oneness with God and feel that you and the divine nature of God are one within the energy, within the reality, within the vibrational field of the divine quality with which you are working. Let God fill you with the spiritual reality of the divine trait with which you are working.

- For example—Let's say that you are working on feeling and realizing the divine ideal of the personality of God using the second day's exercise—*I live each day as a creative divine adventure!*

- As you intuitively surrender to God's special and unique way of revealing this truth to you, you intuitively sense an inner awareness of expansiveness about your life that you have never felt before. Then within this inner realization of really *knowing* that you have infinite possibilities for living a fulfilled life, you rest in and become one with the energy, the reality of this truth, for five to ten minutes.

- Remember that the Presence of God's truth within you is oftentimes experienced as an inner awareness of the nature of God, expressed as a feeling or an emotional impression, of all possibilities and positiveness that is completely free of any negative feelings of restriction or limitation.

Step Four—Slowly Return

- Slowly return to the world about you and put into action the reality of the ideal of God's personality, which you have just been experiencing. Now, work on using the insight that you achieved in your mediation period in your outer activities during the day. Actually and actively, put the reality of the realization of your oneness with the divine quality that you have just worked with into action.

- For example—Let's say that during your meditation time, you were working with the divine ideal of the personality of God using *the fourth day's exercise—I live each day fully alive with divine enthusiasm!*

- First, as you come out of your meditation, you feel divine enthusiasm to such a high degree that you become acutely aware that you are actually looking forward to experiencing the ecstasy that is contained within the day that is before you! You find yourself living the day as one who is fully energized by the expectancy of unlimited fulfillment to be demonstrated throughout your daily experience! And you are naturally filled with a high level of enthusiasm that easily anticipates miracles happening in your life whenever something appears to go wrong during the day!

- Remember that it is your choice about how you are going to live each day of your life. It is up to you to decide that you are the one that is responsible for how you are going to feel throughout the day before you. This day, and every day, choose to be the spiritual truth of who you really are, as one who is made in the perfect image and likeness of God!

TRUTH PRINCIPLES OF MYSTICAL UNION MEDITATION

• You can easily and freely accept all of the high and noble divine qualities of God as your own because you are made in the image and likeness of God. It is your divine birthright to be and show forth the perfection that you are created to be. Your divine birthright of perfection has been created by the supreme wisdom of the Creative Mind of God, combined with the unconditional love of the Heart of God. The divine image of who you really are has always been, is now, and always will be an image of your unlimited, infinite, and eternal perfection, which is forever held within the Mind, the Heart, and the Consciousness of God.

• You can easily join with the truth of who you are by fully accepting that you are, indeed, made in the perfect image and likeness of God. Accept that God created you to express all of the glory that God is. Accept that you are the unique instrument through which the magnificent Presence of God is seen and expressed to the world.

• The divine truths that you focus on in meditation you, become. The divine truth that you focus on in meditation counteracts whatever false beliefs about yourself that you may have mistakenly accepted.

• As you work within yourself in deep contemplative meditation, each and every day, let the truth of God's Presence within your heart and mind filter fully into all the deep recesses of your personality. Let yourself be transformed into the living image and likeness of all that God is. In daily expression, let your life be a living testimony to the magnificence of your true God-Self-Reality.

And So It Is

2

Spiritualize Your Belief System And Improve Your Life

Author's note: The following lesson has been personally worked with and divinely interpreted from the truth of the teachings of Christ, which reveal the following realities of our Divine Selfhood.

As you believe in your heart, so are you.

Live in the world but do not be a part of this world's faulty belief system of personal lack and limitation.

Transform your life into a spiritually great life through the spiritualizing of your belief system via the upliftment of your thoughts.

O ur personal human-based belief system is a composite of all that this world, *our parents, grandparents, family, friends, peer group, neighborhood, era and generation of the time of our birth into this world, heritage and traditions which are contained within the race or nationally into which we were born, and our religion,* has contributed to the personal beliefs of our thoughts and emotions. These beliefs that have come to us from the outside world filter, through our own personality, through our conscious to our subconscious minds. These human-based beliefs, which are based on the beliefs of society, have now given to us a picture of *how to* live our everyday experience. This picture that the beliefs of this world and society have presented to us throughout our lives since the day of our birth may be true or may be false.

When we reach the time in our lives when we realize that we are much more than our previous, human-based beliefs—which may be true or false—then the fun begins! For now we can work with a clear mind and with a spiritualized curriculum for clearing out the beliefs that no longer work, and the ushering in the new belief system that does work for us—or in better terms—the bringing into our awareness the perfect and true belief system of God.

The beliefs that we have set up for ourselves put into automatic operation the images of what we believe we are or what we believe we should be. This can be the true belief system about ourselves that we have gained from God, which is for our *highest good*—or it can be a belief system that is based on our own limited and false view of ourselves, which stems from the beliefs of our own personal limited self.

The possibility for personal fulfillment in this life is contained within the way in which we view ourselves and our lives, based on our belief system about who we believe ourselves to be and how we believe our life will turn out. We can greatly upgrade the quality of our lives through spiritual knowledge or awareness that we have obtained through daily spiritual study and practice, which correspondingly influences the way that we view ourselves, the lives that we are now living, and the lives that we envision for ourselves in the future.

PRINCIPLES AND PRACTICES

Each of you has the capability and the responsibility to shape your life with the highest vision and the greatest knowledge that you have available to you. You gain this true knowledge about yourself and about your life by routinely entering into contemplative-meditative-union with the Presence of God within your heart and mind—who is the Divine Knower of your true spiritualized-personality and the Divine Beholder of your spiritually-perfected life. You then take this inner divine vision of yourself, this spiritually-perfect picture of your life, and you accept it as your one and only true reality. You put this magnificent vision of your true God-Self-Reality into practice each and every day through your spiritualized beliefs about who you are and about the divine significance of your life.

You put your best self-image into action by looking, really looking deeply within yourself, into the innermost level of your psyche to see what qualities of character you possess. As you do so, honestly look at the image of your human self, your everyday personality, and define your dominant qualities. Then look at the perfect image of your true God-Self-Reality who is made in the perfect image and likeness of God and define these priceless qualities. As you compare the two images of who you believe yourself to be, discern which qualities, within your human personality, need to be let go of or changed. Keep what is right and pure within yourself, and then be disciplined enough to let go of what is false and less than who you are as a spiritual being living a spiritual life here on earth—a spiritualized life which is the Heavenly Kingdom of God having taken visible form right here and now.

Listen, listen, listen, for the yearnings of your heart telling you about the majestic spiritual-being you were created to be. Develop a belief system about yourself and about your life, which will help you to be the expression of the exquisite, magnificent God-Self that you are. And by so doing, you will be forever without the pain of being human and living a life of insignificance.

When you really know, when you faithfully and steadfastly believe, that God is the one and only power for good in your life, then you are living your life by the belief system of God. When you really believe that God is the one and only source of real unconditional love in your life, then you are emotionally living your everyday life by the belief system of God. When you know that God is the ever-present source of all of the wisdom that you will ever have need of in your life, then you are living the truth of the belief system of God. When you base the foundation of your belief system on God's truth, you are living God's life and God's reality.

On an everyday level you essentially create the quality and tone of your day through your belief about how the day before you is going to be. If you believe that today is God's day filled with God's goodness, beauty, and fulfillment, then it will be! If you believe that you will be happy all day long and if you are really committed to feeling that way, then you will! If you believe that you can do all things through the Presence of God living and working through you, then you will!

On a higher level, several physicists who have worked extensively with quantum physics have theorized that the outer picture of what we literally see in this world is the product of our inner belief system; a outer world-reality founded on a collective belief system that is based on what we *believe* our outer reality will be. In essence, what we see is what we believe we will see. This is also a common theme that appears repeatedly within many, if not all, of the major religious writings and belief systems. This being so—what we believe reality to be, within our minds, becomes the actuality of our outer reality—it then benefits us greatly if we take the time and effort to enter into thoughtful inner contemplation and perceive what our current beliefs about ourselves and our lives are. It will empower us greatly to let go of a belief system that is not to our spiritual liking and to choose a belief system that believes that God, the supreme Creator of All-good, is in complete and absolute control of who we are and of the true reality of our world.

Live this life to the fullest. Know and believe with all of your heart that you have a great purpose here on earth. Know and believe with an inner surety what that purpose is to outwardly be; express, manifest, represent, and reflect the spiritual perfection and magnificence which you become consciously aware of when you have achieved inward union with the Presence of God within your heart and mind.

STEPS TO TAKE AND PRINCIPLES TO WORK WITH TO CLEAR UP YOUR LIMITED INNER BELIEF SYSTEM

Upgrade your belief system by contemplating and working with the following exercises that are contained within this extremely important lesson. Work with these spiritually transformative exercises for a week, a month, or for however long you feel intuitively guided to do so, until the absolute of spiritual transformation has taken place within yourself and within your life. Most importantly of all, work with this lesson periodically throughout your entire life, so that you will always be the divine perfection that you were created to be!

- Every day, take note to really look around you and realize that the world that you see is made up of the belief systems of those around you—the beliefs of people from the beginning of time and the beliefs of people in the present. Realize that your life experience is also made up of your own beliefs that you have brought forth into visible manifestation.

- Spend at least a week, and periodically during your life, to pay close attention to each thought you have which defines a belief that you have about yourself and your life. For example: As you go through your day, do you believe that disease is more the norm in your life then health? Do you believe that you are unloving and/or unlovable? Perhaps you believe that life is stressful and lacks real joy and happiness. Maybe you even believe that you are not talented enough to be successful within a chosen career, although you truly desire to give your best so that this world is a better world because of your efforts and talents.

- List each belief as you have them during the day. Carry a notebook with you and write your beliefs down or write them down at the end of the day.

- With each belief that you have written down, ask yourself if that specific belief is created or founded upon the belief system of God! Remember that the belief system of God is based on the following truths.

  God is the one and only power of All-good and absolute fulfillment.

  God is the one and only presence of true unconditional love, and the presence of God's unconditional love is always with you.

  God is the supreme wisdom of the universe, which keeps this world in divine order, and you are one with the All-Knowing Mind of God.

  Also be aware that the false belief system of this world is based on the false assumption that we are separated from God's Presence.

- Remember at all times that God is the core, the center, and the nucleus of who we are when we sincerely love God with our whole mind, heart, soul, and being. When we believe as God believes, we start to live a life of divine perfection, which is God's plan for us.

- Ask yourself the following question about each belief that you have written down from the day just past: *Which belief system am I believing in and living my life by—this world's belief in separation from God or God's belief system of eternal unity?* When you have your answer, simply let go of the beliefs that are spiritually untrue. You can also redefine the false beliefs into the spiritual truth, as explained in the following exercise.

- Make a list of the limited and restrictive belief systems of this world in which you live. List every repressive and self-limiting belief, which you feel that your immediate world believes. For example—*The world in which I live believes that supply and income are dependent on having a job and on the good-will of the person for which I am working.*

- Take each one of these restrictive and oppressive beliefs into a quiet state of mind and relaxation, redefine it by your own spiritual truth and insight, and then write it down. For example—*My joy is to be living the very reality of God in expression, and it is the very Presence of God who leads me to my rightful place (job) of expression. It is the All-supply of the universal Mind of God that supplies my every need.*

- Redefine every false belief of this world, which is comprised of the false beliefs in lack and limitation, and make the new belief system a part of yourself and your reality by daily studying these new God-Self-Realized principles of spiritually-based, unlimited fulfillment until they become a real part of your life-reality.

- Make a list of all of your personal beliefs about yourself and your life right now, which are restrictive and confining in nature. For example—*I am nothing without a mate.*

- Redefine each one of these restrictive personal beliefs by the inner truth that is revealed to you in a quiet time of inner contemplation between yourself and God's presence. For example—*I am the very expression of God made manifest in physical form. I am complete and whole because of who I am spiritually. I will draw to me those who are also whole and complete within themselves, so that I and all others who are drawn into my life may be a blessing to all concerned.*

- As you work with your beliefs you will find that many of them are without power or spiritual principle—thus they can easily be dropped and redefined into life-giving, fulfillment-directed principles to be lived.

MEDITATION

Meditation is a practice by which you actually join with the Presence of God within your heart and mind for a time of inner awakening, through which you will achieve the inner awareness that you are, in fact, made in the perfect image and likeness of God right here and right now. But, you must know this experience, this reality, first hand. And this can only be achieved by the art of meditating on the reality of God, joining with the very energy, the vibration of God, within the center of your heart and mind, and then bringing that joining of energy and vibration to your conscious mind and life, so that you are now the living example of all that God is, dressed within the glorious form that you inhabit.

MEDITATION AND VISUALIZATION PRACTICE

The following meditation and visualization practice will be used to bring about a clearing process within your body, mind, and Soul so that you can "rest within a state of inner clarity," and by so doing, you will find that you will be better able to redefine your inner and outer belief system, and you can begin the re-creation of who you really are. By daily establishing yourself within a state of consciousness which is free from all of the false programming and beliefs of this world, you will find yourself in an "unfettered and clear" state of mind and emotion which, in turn, will enable you to be a clear transmitter of spiritual truth to yourself and to the world around you.

BEGINNING OF THE MEDITATION PRACTICE

- **Rest**—become still within your body and your mind. Prepare yourself to experience a transformational, meditative exercise, which will create a greater condition of inner clarity within yourself. You will then be in a mental and emotional state, which is ready to receive the belief system of God. The belief system of God knows that you are already whole and complete within yourself, and you will experience this in proportion to your conscious realized oneness with the Presence of God within your heart and mind.

- **Completely rest**—within a deep sense of inner calmness and peace. In your mind's eye, in your imaginative ability, bring your attention within yourself to your heart-center, and feel the beating of your heart and the slow inhalation and exhalation of your breath for a few minutes. With your attention on yourself, feel yourself centered within your heart-center. Your heart is the spiritual center of the spiritual reality of your true God-Self-Reality. Realize that you have within yourself a spiritually mature adult, your true God-Self, who is always aware of your spiritual truth—a spiritual truth, that in your oneness with the Presence of God, you are completely whole and complete within yourself. Remember that your true God-Self is always ready, willing, and able to guide you to the realization of your true God-Self identity.

- **As you sit**—within your heart-center, in union with your true God-Self, feel your heart expand with unconditional love for God, for yourself, and for your life. Just sit and feel your heart-center expand with unconditional love.

- **Now repeat**—to yourself silently, slowly, and repeatedly the following "Statement of Truth" for three to five minutes, or longer if you desire. This statement of truth is a divine truth of who you really are within your realized oneness with the Presence of God that resides within your heart-center. As you focus on the following statements of spiritual truth, you will intuitively become these spectacular truths on which you are focusing.

I And God Are One

- **As you slowly**—repeat this truth to yourself you will become increasingly aware that you are indeed one with the Presence of God. In fact, in time, you will come to know that you have always been one with the Presence of God and that you will always be one with the Presence of God throughout eternity!

- **Now repeat**—to yourself the following statement of truth for three to five minutes, or however long you desire, to yourself slowly, silently, and repeatedly until you feel yourself becoming the spiritual reality of the truth on which you are focused.

All That God Is I Am

- **As you repeat**—this statement of truth repeatedly to yourself, you will find that the divine nature of God—expressed as self-confidence, fearlessness, an inner knowingness of wholeness, completeness, and unconditional love for yourself, others, and life—is now yours.

- **Finally repeat**—to yourself the following statement of truth for three to five minutes, or however long you desire, to yourself slowly, silently and repeatedly until you feel yourself becoming the spiritual reality of the truth on which you are focused.

I Am Now Whole And Complete Within Myself

- **As you repeat**—this statement of truth repeatedly to yourself, you will finally know that you are indeed whole and complete within yourself without the need for anyone or anything outside of yourself to fulfill you. You now realize that you no longer need anyone outside of yourself to tell you how wonderful and great you are—you already are wonderful and great because of your oneness with the Presence of God within your heart and mind. You no longer have the need to have outer roles of being a mother, father, spouse, or any role of importance in the secular world to fill you with a sense of importance and worthiness. You are already spiritually important, worthy, and whole and complete within yourself!

VISUALIZATION EXERCISE

- **Rest**—completely within the inner quietness and calmness of your *spiritual heart-center*, your True-God-Self-Reality which is always in an inner state of contentment and satisfaction, thus allowing yourself an intimate experience of inner clarity within the *Healing White Light Presence and Reality of God*—at the center of your mind, heart, and body.

- **As you rest**—deeper and deeper within yourself, bring your attention to your heart-center by focusing on the serene and even beating of your heart. Feel as if the Heart of God were literally beating within your body. Really feel your oneness with the unconditionally loving Presence of God within the center of your heart and feeling nature.

- **In an inner state**—of peace and self-contentment within your heart-center, imagine that you are being filled with the *Healing-White-Light of God's Presence*, filling and flowing throughout your entire body temple.

  When your eye is single, meaning that your heart and mind are focused on realizing the Presence of God, your whole body will literally be filled with Light.

If you have a predominately visualizing nature—see or imagine seeing the Healing-White-Light fill your entire body, and peacefully become one with the Healing-White-Light of God's Presence until your awareness of yourself lessens and only the Healing-White-Light becomes your reality.

If you have a predominately feeling nature—as you visualize the Healing-White-Light within your imagination, simultaneously experience the heartfelt feelings of inner love, peace, and contentment. Experience these feelings as the true essence of the Healing-White-Light of God's Presence. Become one with the Healing-White-Light essence of inner love, peace, and contentment until the human *you* no longer exists and you literally find yourself becoming the absolute nature of love, peace, and contentment.

If you have a predominately intellectual nature—know and contemplate that the Healing-White-Light that you see within your imagination is the pure essence and Presence of God being revealed as enlightened truth. The enlightened truth that recognizes the one and only power of God—the enlightened truth that sees God as the one and only Presence—the enlightened truth that acknowledges God as the one and only wisdom keeps you and your life in perfect divine order.

Pick which nature you feel predominately at ease and in union with—visual, emotional, or intellectual. Or work with all three natures, one at a time, or all at one sitting, for a holistically-balanced visualization exercise.

Keep sitting for a space of time in this continual energy flow of clearing, cleansing, purifying, and healing White-Light of God's Presence of wholeness, completeness, and divine flawlessness and purity. Let God's Healing-White-Light flow over and around you until you feel free, clear and whole, with a feeling of tingling and energizing energy flowing throughout your body—surrounding you and filling your whole being.

CONCLUSION OF THE MEDITATION AND VISUALIZATION PRACTICE

• When you look within yourself with your mind's eye—your intuitive nature—and you see and feel inner clarity—inner peace—inner contentment—then allow God's Presence to sit with you in this beautiful clear state and really commune with the Presence of God within your heart-center.

Feel your oneness with the inner peace of God's Presence.

Feel yourself being filled with the Wisdom of God.

Feel yourself being loved by the Love of God.

Feel yourself being cared for and cherished by the Presence of God.

And rest in that splendor.

• Now slowly come out of the meditation and visualization practice knowing that each time that you use the above meditation and visualization, a clearing process has been brought into practice in a very easy, peaceful, and proper manner.

Know that whatever needed transformation, major change, clearing out, or healing within your belief system has now taken place, to the degree that you were able to be completely relaxed and open to the Presence of God and the healing truth of God, to bring about change within your heart and mind.

This meditation and visualization practice, along with doing the spiritual practices contained within this lesson will, in time, completely re-establish within you the belief system of spiritual reality. You will be inwardly guided to remake your mind-set one of positiveness, strength, and hope-filled.

PRINCIPLES THAT COMPRISE OUR BELIEF SYSTEMS

The roles that we take on in this life are made up of the combined beliefs and influences of ourselves, our parents, our society, and the lessons that we brought with us to this life experience to accelerate our own spiritual growth and the spiritual growth of others.

- The person that we are now is the one that we have created from the previous viewpoint of our life experience.

- We are subject to change at any point of time, when we decide to change the inner picture that we hold of ourselves.

- We are also open to change when we meditate daily, when we open up our hearts and minds to the inner influence of spiritual reality that we hold deep within ourselves—deep within the inner recesses of our consciousness.

- This energy vibration of who we are spiritually, and the true roles that we are to play out in this lifetime, are brought into focus within our conscious minds when we see clearly, the divine picture of our True-God-Self in meditation. For it is during meditation that we turn away from all the outer programming of who we think we are, and we turn inward to the true God-Reality of our true Beingness—the Beingness of God taking hold of this life experience through our conscious interaction with God.

- Yes, we are the image and likeness of God right here and right now but it takes a clear mind to grasp this picture of our True-God-Self (*totally*). That is why we study, meditate, and question our thinking processes from day to day.

- Be clear about what you are doing and why you are doing it. Gain your direction in life from the supreme director of your life—God—and then you will know, without a doubt, that that self that you are aware of, each and every day, is the True-God-Self that you really are.

• With every step that you take when you have intentionally joined daily in meditation with the Presence of God, which is always abiding within you, then do you know without a doubt that the place where upon you stand is *Holy Ground*. Then do you know that you are a divine expression of God here on earth, living the life that you are meant to live to the fullest.

• Every thought that you think is constantly creating the reality of who you are in outer form and expression. So you see how important it is to gain the inner knowingness of who you are as a *Perfect Spiritual Being*, so that you will *from moment to moment* shape within your thought system the thoughts and beliefs that create the True-Spiritual-Mold, the True-Heavenly-Image of your true and Highest-God-Self!

• As you ready yourself to come unto the Holy Shrine of your God-Self-Reality in meditation daily, come unto yourself with an inner sense of worship and reverence for who you are. Take this sense of worthiness into your *Inner-Heart-Shrine-Center* within yourself, and there give praise and gratitude for the glorious spiritual *Light* that you are.

• Be determined to live out this *Perfect Divine Vision* of who you are in your day-to-day experiences and then you will feel fulfilled, and you will have a life in which there is true meaning to the roles and images that you do express and embody.

DAILY MEDITATION EXERCISES
BEING THE SPIRITUAL ROLE MODEL THAT
YOU WERE CREATED TO BE
MOURNING EXERCISE

In your daily morning meditation take quiet, special time for yourself and join in oneness with the Presence of God within your heart and mind, and through the Presence of God within your heart and mind.

Really see yourself through your Creator's eyes

See the true beauty and the wonderful work of divine art that you are.

See the love that fills your heart to over-flowing.

See the great works that you have before you to do in this life.

Within this meditation, really see the over-all greatness of who you are as the embodiment of the presence, the love, the wisdom of God. Realize and acknowledge your divine magnificence. Really see yourself as God sees you—as the divine creation of God, the product of God's great unconditional love taking visible form, as You.

Know Who You Are—

After this morning's meditation, be sure to take with you *throughout the day* the image of your True-God-Self-Reality that you just experienced in your meditation.

- **Act**—as the Presence of God within you would act.

- **Talk**—as the Presence of God within you would talk.

- **See others**—as the Presence of God within you would see them.

Perform every activity before you as the Presence of God *within you* would perform.

- **Love**—the way that God would love.

- **Give**—the way that God would give.

- **Feel**—the way that God would feel.

- **See the best**—in this life the way that God would see the best.

VISUALIZATION EXERCISE

Hold before you in the quiet, lovely, and peaceful center of your Being, the picture of who you want to be. See yourself as loving, giving, strong, peaceful, fulfilled, and filled with divine wisdom.

As you view the self that you really want to be without any feeling of doubt or judgment, feel yourself merge with that inner perfect picture—and as you and your True-Self become one—rest and experience how it feels to be this Real-God-Self.

Remember that we become the embodiment of who we believe we are. So the more that we become one with our true Spiritual-Self in meditation, *during our times of inner visualization and in our thought process,* then do we become that perfect image of Self, for which we are seeking.

BELIEF SYSTEMS
OUR DAILY ROLES IN REGARD TO OUR LIVING UP TO OUR BELIEF SYSTEMS

Daily Exercise—Letting Go of Restrictive Roles

- Spend a week, a month, or however long you feel intuitively guided to work with this spiritually healing process. Also use this extremely important exercise for self-transformation periodically during your life, for continually-expanded spiritual growth.

- Spend this study time letting go, *within your mind,* of the roles that you have been performing in your life.

- Remember—you are not the roles that you play in this lifetime.

For Example—If one of your roles is being a wife or husband—let go of that role *in your mind* by knowing that, if you were not a wife or husband that you would still be who you are spiritually. Now contemplate who you would be and how you would feel if you were single? Realize that you are who you are spiritually, which is one who is whole and complete, regardless of the roles of being a wife or husband that you play. In reality, you bring the fullness of your spiritually perfect and whole God-Self into the active role of being a wife or husband. The actual role of being a wife or husband does not make you whole and complete. You are spiritually whole and complete already, regardless of the roles that you decide to play in this lifetime.

- Each day, *a little step at a time,* let go of the roles and the titles that you have given to yourself and that others have given to you to define who you are.

- Try being without an outer human identity—and work on knowing yourself as a unique, perfect, and complete spiritual-reflection of God in form and expression.

- Realize that you are the perfect manifestation of God who is being guided and directed by the inner Presence of God to your highest fulfillment, with regard to the activities and roles with which you are to be involved.

- Just *Be* and you will find yourself being more than you have ever imagined being!

HEALING MEDITATION

- I enter into the inner framework of who I am in the inner chamber of my heart, and here I rest in the Divine Presence of God within my heart and Soul—saying—

- To you—Father-Mother God—I offer up the human everyday reality of who I think I am.

- I completely and freely let go of all the images—beliefs—and ideas that I hold in my mind of who I think I am.

- And I now rest in the inner Light of Knowingness—the Center-Soul-Reality of who I really am—and here I commune with the God-Self that I was created to be before the beginning of time.

- Here I recognize that I was created as a Soul-Presence of an aspect of God who is the real inner element of who I really am.

- In the inner garden of my Soul—I plant the seed-thought of Spiritual-Being-ness as the image of who I am, that will grow to complete maturity in this life-time, so that I may be a living expression of the presence and personality of God, so intimately, that I actually become that God-Presence.

- Today I consider myself to be the greatest blessing that I could be to myself by realizing that I am more than I ever thought that I was, and I am now deter-mined to live that Self to the fullest and to the best of my abilities.

- I surrender myself as living proof that God is indeed alive and well (here), within the Self that I am.

- Today I will live the glory that God is to the fullest, and I consider it a privilege to be called the Image of God.

- Dear Father-Mother God—I rest in the bosom of your heart, knowing that because of our oneness I will, forevermore, be a Light unto this world that I live in because You are always with me.

                                                                And So It I

3

The Limitless Manifestation

Author's note: The following lesson has been personally worked with and divinely interpreted from the truth of the teachings of Christ, which reveal the following realities of our Divine Selfhood.

Whoever already has a consciousness, an awareness, of having All-good things necessary for fulfillment, to them shall be given, and they shall have more abundance in their lives. But whoever has an awareness of not having, from them will be taken away even that which they do have because of their own restrictive nature of non-appreciation.

Today is the day, today is the life, which God has made; let us appreciate, rejoice, and be glad in it. For the earth and your life are God's perfect creations, and within God's perfect creations, all fulfillment already exists.

Your body is the perfect temple of the living Presence of God which is in you. The body temple in which you live has been created for you out of God's Consciousness of love and perfection, and this perfect body temple is to be appreciated and honored for the magnificent holy work of art that it is!

Love one another through the healing power of appreciation. As God continually and unconditionally appreciates and loves us, so should we also love and appreciate one another, thus healing all that is less than loving within ourselves and within others.

Whatever actions you take, whatever work you do, do all with the limitless manifestation-power of appreciation, do all to the glory of God, do all to the magnificence of the living Presence of God's Perfection expressing through you.

Study Note: Because of the magnitude and significance of the important content of this essential study material, I would suggest that you spend quality time for one to two weeks, a month or more, or however long it takes you to transform a limited focus towards life into an unrestricted expansive state of creative con-

sciousness, which is always open to the unlimited Consciousness of God to create through.

THE EXPANSIVE POWER OF APPRECIATION

L earning to use the expansive-power of appreciation, learning to use the tremendous, limitless manifestation-power of appreciation in the right way, is one of the most useful lessons that you can work with and incorporate into your life experience. This is a lesson, which will add to your everyday life a fullness and a richness that is beyond measure.

When you think and say the word "*appreciation*" to yourself, you convey an emotionally charged vision to your psyche, which in turn, is a tremendous manifestation-power, a creative force, that signals your mind to think thoughts that give you permission, that allow you to have an abundance of health, love, and prosperity in your life in an unlimited amount. When you think or say the word appreciation, you start an emotional *supervision* within your consciousness that says to your creative mind—

I am now ready to create more of what it is that I already have appreciation for—in abundance!

The inappropriate use of the power of appreciation, or the opposite/restrictive use of the power of appreciation, is found in the daily habit of feeling the feelings of ingratitude and non-appreciation, and in the thinking of thoughts of ingratitude and non-appreciation. The wrong use of the feelings and thoughts of ingratitude and non-appreciation make up most of the problems that you find in your life right now.

- **Non-Appreciation for Your Body**—can be one of the main ingredients found in the misuse of your body and in the feelings of stress that may fill your body, which contributes to various diseases that you may experience. Work each day on thanking your body for being a perfect and useful vehicle through which to express.

- **Non-Appreciation for Your Relationionships**—may blind you to the beauty that you now have with another. Be in a continual state of appreciation for every relationship that you have now, or have had in the past, or that you will have in the future. For each relationship is a treasure map of information about yourself and the places within your psyche that need improvement.

- **Non-Appreciation for Life**—can cause restrictive thoughts that you retain within your mind about your life, which can hold you back from really living a life that is filled with the creative genius of God creating—through your life—demonstrations of sacredness and specialness. Ingratitude and non-appreciation for your life is the main cause of thoughts and feelings of hope-lessness and despair, which are a complete waste of precious time and life. Develop a healthy sense of appreciation for the invaluable life that you have been given. Each day is a divine gift in which you can live out a life of hope and excitement about living a better life each and every day!

- **Non-Appreciation for Your Job**—is found in the feelings of having a com-plete disregard for a job well done. Ingratitude and non-appreciation for your work is a waste of time, for your work life takes up a large amount of the time that you spend *existing* during your life. When you have a feeling of apprecia-tion for your work, you are filled with a 100% commitment to doing a job well, which fills you with a feeling of accomplishment and purpose.

As you can see, the development of the divine quality and expression of apprecia-tion within yourself is one of the most useful abilities that you can spend your time developing. Using and developing the expansive manifestation-power of appreciation opens up your awareness to the acceptance of living a life that is open to, and ready to receive, all possibilities for expanded and abundant fulfill-ment.

PRINCIPLES TO WORK WITH
DURING THIS SPECIAL TIME OF STUDY

The human feelings and thoughts of ingratitude and non-appreciation are the result of the human, false, limited belief in scarcity.

- The false human belief in scarcity tells us that everything that *appears* to us, as *being less than perfect* is the truth of the situation, another person, or ourselves. Our false belief in scarcity convinces us that our life situation at the present time is separated from God, separated from our good, or separated from that which is necessary for our fulfillment, survival, and sense of contentment.

- The mistaken belief in scarcity keeps us imprisoned within the false belief sys-tem of *not having*. When we believe in, and focus on, the false belief system of *not having,* we create more of *not having* within our lives, and we falsely accept that the negative lifestyle of *not having* is the natural state of our life.

• When we are believing in and living within the false belief system of *not having,* we have literally closed off our vision from all we do have and what we could potentially have, thus creating a life experience of even greater lack and desperation of limitation. Hopefully, you can easily see that living within this false belief of *not having* is not the way to live, nor is it the way to rise above the false belief of scarcity.

• The false thought-system of scarcity is a manmade thought-system that has been created out of the false belief of separation from the unconditional love of God. When we live within the false belief system of scarcity, we are blind to the truth of *God's ever-available abundance everywhere present.* Within the false emotional state of ingratitude and non-appreciation, we find that we are incapable of being *one with* the Spiritual Perception of God—Who perceives and sees only the perfect and beautiful creation and visions of God's *Magnificent Heart* made manifest as this world.

DIVINE LAW OF APPRECIATION
EQUALS
DIVINE LAW OF ABUNDANCE

The unconditional love of God has already given to you all that you need for your own unique demonstration and showing forth a perfectly wonderful life.

The *"Divine Law of Appreciation"* means that we have accepted within ourselves, and into our life experience, the truth that knows that God has already provided for us all that we could ever have need of for our complete fulfillment and happiness. Our daily expression of appreciation for *all of our needs already being taken care of by the unconditionally loving Presence of God,* within your hearts and minds, frees us from the false belief in scarcity.

This world, this universe, and all that is and has life are created from the Consciousness of God that knows only *unlimited abundance of all good things.* In proportion to our daily ability to recognize, accept, and remember this wonderful truth, then will we be in the position of outwardly seeing and experiencing the abundance of God in our own lives.

EXERCISES

Transforming the limiting emotional energy of non-appreciation into the abundance-producing emotional energy of appreciation

Each day of your life from now on, it is extremely important that you be thankful in all seen and unseen good, and in all yet to be manifested and realized good, because the unconditional, All-Knowing love of God has already provided the very best for you. From this day forward, accept that you are constantly surrounded by the abundant atmosphere of the unlimited Consciousness of God. This universe in which we live, move, and have our being is an infinite atmosphere or divine awareness of *infinite fulfillment and divine order*—and always available, and in inexhaustible abundance. This incredibly unfathomable, exceptional, rich with divine gifts beyond our wildest dreams—Divine Universe in which we Live—is literally the Consciousness of God. You actually live every moment of your life within God's Consciousness of abundance and within the unconditionally loving and caring awareness of the Heart and Mind of God, which knows that—*All good things that are necessary for your ultimate fulfillment are already yours.* Through your awareness of *All good things that are necessary for your ultimate fulfillment are already yours,* you bring into visible manifestation the abundance that already surrounds you.

For Example—Let us say that you and your best friend both love roses and you are both walking within a beautiful garden filled with the vast beauty and sweet-scented fragrance of roses. You, personally, are extremely aware of and have a deep inner appreciation for the splendor of the roses that surround you. You freely and openly invite the pleasure and enjoyment of the beauty and abundance of life into the center of your being through the experience of the walk that you are taking in the rose garden. You feel exuberantly and lavishly alive, you feel inwardly and outwardly healed, rejuvenated, and renewed within the richness of nature. But your friend, on the other hand, is very upset about an earlier argument that she had with her loved one. Your friend is not only unaware of the beauty of the roses that surround her, but she may even be upset with you, because of your blissful countenance which originates from your awareness of the beauty of nature that currently encompasses you. From this example, you can easily recognize that we are all surrounded by God's universal beauty and abundance. Every day we have the choice either to be aware of the splendor that surrounds us, or to close off our thoughts and emotions to the magnificence of

God's creation through our own negative thinking and acceptance of lack and limitation.

Having continual awareness and openness to the gifts of life that surround you is the gateway to accepting the abundance of all that you have need of—from moment to moment—for your own unique manifestation of fulfillment that has already been provided for you from a most loving God. As you take your daily walk along the path of life, be aware of the abundance that God has already prepared for you. Walk along your life's path in a living state of *Divine Grace*. Within the following exercise you will find out *how to* walk along this extraordinary path of *Divine Grace*—unceasingly.

Through working weekly with the following exercises, we easily become aware of what it is that we are complaining about and, thus, greatly restricting our lives through the negative emotional energy of ingratitude and non-appreciation. When we change, heal, and transform that negativity into acceptance of the abundance that already surrounds us, we create an inner and outer atmosphere of contentment and fulfillment. Work with each exercise for as long as you feel intuitively guided to do so—and in the future, return to these important exercises whenever you find yourself complaining about anything in your life.

FIRST HEALING EXERCISE

- Become still and feel your oneness with the completeness of the Presence of God that is within the center of your heart and mind.

- Feel your oneness with the wisdom and understanding of God.

- In a relaxed state of honesty ask yourself—What do I find myself complaining about, in my daily life experience, the majority of the time?

    Perhaps you are always complaining about a certain relationship or perhaps you are always complaining about your relationships, regardless of who they are? Perhaps you complain about your work or the person with whom you work? Do you find yourself complaining about your state of health, more than you would like? Are you critical about your body, or your weight, or your looks in general? Do you find yourself being critical about the personalities of others? Do you find yourself complaining about the excessive business pressures of your life? Are you feeling restricted about where you live? Do you find yourself resenting the fact that you seem to be doing the will of others instead of following the Divine Will of God for your life and pursuing your desire to fulfill yourself on a personal level and spiritually?

- Take this area of complaint and intentionally stop focusing on it. Remind yourself that, that which you focus on and give emotional attention to, you tend to create more of in your life. When you are paying attention to and focusing on a lack in your life, you are making that false lack real instead of knowing within your heart and mind that God has already provided for your abundant fulfillment. Remember, and continually affirm to yourself, that this perceived lack in your life is just an illusion of the erroneous belief of this world that believes in, and puts power into, the false acceptance of scarcity. Refuse to believe in this false belief of scarcity anymore! Be done with wasting your precious life feeling bad about something that is a spiritual lie about your life. The spiritual truth has now come into your life so that you can really start to live life more abundantly, free from the fear of all lack and limitation.

PRINCIPLES FOR HEALING ALL FALSE COMPLAINTS

The following suggestions are extremely important to work with on a daily basis! Study, contemplate, and think about these principles for healing all false complaints until they become a natural way of thinking.

- **Refuse to think about** the false complaint anymore. Each time that you think about the false complaint, you are literally giving it power. You are giving it reality because you are believing in it as real. Take the false power of this false complaint out of your life completely by refusing to give it any more attention within the creative realm of your thoughts. Whenever you find yourself thinking about this false complaint—**tell yourself**—I refuse to think about this false complaint anymore! I refuse to give it reality within myself and within my life! I just don't want it anymore! I don't believe in it anymore! It has no power over me anymore!

- **Refuse to feel** any fear, resentment, or frustration about the false complaint. Whenever you give emotional attention to a false complaint, you are dramatically making that false complaint real to yourself. When we give in to feeling negative, fearful, and restrictive emotions about a false complaint we tend to become immersed within the energy of that emotion, and may even find ourselves living in the atmosphere of that negative emotion for days at a time.

When we refuse to give life and validity to the false complaint by refusing to feel negatively about it, we are spiritually turning our back on a lie about ourselves, about our life, and about others. Whenever you find yourself feeling negatively about this false complaint—**tell yourself**—I refuse to feel negatively about this false complaint anymore! I refuse to give it reality within myself and within my life by being in a continual calm state of non-reaction, of neutrality, of being an innocent observer! I don't want to feel that way anymore! I don't believe in it anymore! It has no power over me!

• **Refuse**, as much as possible, to talk to others about the false complaint. Whenever we complain to another about a personal sense of scarcity in our lives, we are literally joining with another to make this false belief in scarcity a greater reality in our life. Now we have another person who is seeing us as a victim of limited circumstances, who feels the same feelings of fear about our life as we do. We now have a co-creative partner who believes that there is a principle of lack, limitation, and scarcity working in our life that is greater than the law of God's All-goodness and All-power. Needless to say, this is not what we want to do! We want to be free of the belief in the false concept of scarcity, and this will be more difficult to do if we have intentionally made up a group of people who support us in our false belief of scarcity, lack, and limitation.

Please note: If you feel that you must speak to someone about your area of complaint, be sure to speak with a counselor, minister, healing practitioner, trusted friend or confidant who will support you in your desire to realize God's positive power to heal the area that represents a problem in your life.

Now Visualize—how you look and feel—being free of this area of complaint in your life. Really feel your freedom from this complaint for as long as you can. The more that you can feel your freedom from any complaint, in proportion, the reality of that complaint in your life will lessen. Visualize how you would feel if that complaint was no longer in your life. Within the spiritual reality of God, the reason for that complaint never was a reality. Within the spiritual reality of who you are, as made in the perfect image and likeness of God, the negative response to the false complaint was never a part of your real spiritualized personality.

• In a relaxed state of honesty ask yourself—What do I appreciate about my life right now?

For Example—Perhaps you are grateful that you have a roof over your head, that you have special items of beauty that have special meaning to you. Perhaps you appreciate that you have friends that are loving and supporting, or that you are surrounded by joyful people. Perhaps you have the ability to visualize a life that is perfect and fulfilled.

- Now focus all of your attention on the feelings of appreciation for what it is that you do love about your life right now. Close your eyes and really allow yourself to feel the love and appreciation for that which you do have, for that which you are genuinely thankful for in your life at this time.

- Whenever you start to feel yourself focusing on the false lack, *instantly* replace that feeling and picture of limitation with the feeling and picture of that which you do appreciate. Replace the false picture of lack with the true manifestation-power of that for which you are grateful in your life.

- When you think about your life, think about those aspects of your life for which you already have appreciation. With every thought that you think, realize that you are co-creating that thought about your life into a very real possibility. So think thoughts about what you already appreciate, thus bringing yourself into oneness with the creative Consciousness of God Who knows only appreciation. Realize that your life is really the *Divine handiwork of God* for which you are the benefactor of all that is beautiful and wondrous. Start to think about your life as a genuine gift of God's unconditional and unlimited love for you.

- Whenever you experience feelings about your life, encourage feelings of appreciation and love for what God has already given to you. Allow your heart to open up to the infinite possibilities that your life holds for you. Stop wasting your valuable time feeling upset about what you do not have and start to emotionally live in God's reality of unlimited fulfillment.

- When you talk to others, talk about that which you have appreciation for in your life. Let others share with you the joy-filled appreciation that you have for your life. Demonstrate that you are living within the Consciousness of God, in which there is only unlimited contentment and satisfaction.

  For further advanced work*—in turning the perception of lack into the perception of fulfillment, work with and heal the following areas of specific complaints. Ask yourself the following questions and follow through with the steps that we have just completed with our first exercise. You may want to do the following exercises all at one time, or you may want to work on each question separately for a period of time that feels comfortable for you.*

SECOND HEALING EXERCISE

- In a relaxed state of honesty **ask yourself**—What do I find myself complaining about, concerning my body, most of the time? *Perhaps you find yourself complaining about your weight, your looks, your age, or a disease.*

- Select the main area of complaint and intentionally stop focusing on it.

- Decline to think about this false complaint anymore.

- Refuse to experience any anxiety, displeasure, or lack of fulfillment because of this false complaint from now on.

- Refuse to converse with others about this false complaint anymore.

Now Visualize—how you would look and feel if you were now free of this area of complaint in your life. Heartily acknowledge that this complaint is no longer an obstacle to your own inner realization of perfection. Visualize how you would live your everyday life experience if this complaint were no longer a reality—for in the spiritual reality of God, the reason for this complaint never was a reality. Visualize yourself living in a body which is one of your greatest and most supportive friends.

- In a relaxed state of honesty ask yourself—What do I appreciate about my body right now?

    For Example—*Perhaps you love the way that your body feels when you are exercising, or that your body has the ability to feel strength. Perhaps you appreciate your eyes, your hair, your skin, or the height of your body temple.*

- Now focus all of your attention on the feelings of appreciation for what it is that you do love about your body. Close your eyes and really allow yourself to feel the love and appreciation for that which you are genuinely thankful for about your body. You may even want to love and appreciate the areas of your body that seem to be less than perfect. By doing this you will change your negative perception about your body, thus allowing your body the chance to heal through the power of appreciation and unconditional love.

- Whenever you start to feel yourself focusing on the false lack, *at once* replace that feeling and picture of limitation with the feeling and picture of that which you do appreciate. Replace the false picture of lack with the true manifestation-power of that which you have appreciation for within your body temple.

- Whenever you think about your body, send the healing thoughts of appreciation to your unique and special body temple. Take time to intellectually acknowledge and appreciate the fact that your body has been created by God so that the Presence of God can live and express through you. Your body is a *Divine Work of Art*, and it deserves to be highly appreciated!

- When you experience feelings about your body, let them be feelings of admiration and honor for the body temple that God's creative Consciousness of perfection has created for you. The emotional feelings of appreciation for the wonderful body temple that you call your home can bring great healing to your body. Feel towards your body as you would towards a loved one whom you respect and cherish more than anyone else in the world. Let your body know how much you love and appreciate it and in return, your body will be a more loving atmosphere for you to live within.

- When you have dialogue with others, talk about that which you are grateful for about your holy body temple. From this day forward, with every word that you speak, promise to yourself to speak only words of love about your body temple. Speak about your body from an attitude of unconditional love and unlimited appreciation.

THIRD HEALING EXERCISE

- In a relaxed state of honesty **ask yourself**—What do I find myself complaining about, concerning another person, most of the time? *Perhaps you find yourself complaining about how another treats you with disrespect or lack of attention, love, appreciation, or recognition.*

- Recognize this area of complaint and immediately stop thinking about it.

- Refuse to give any more attention to this false complaint.

- Adamantly refuse to consider feeling any apprehension, exasperation, or disappointment about this false complaint any longer.

- Do not speak to others about this false complaint from this moment forward.

Now Visualize—how you feel as one who is totally free of this complaint about another in your life. See yourself joyfully celebrating your freedom from this complaint about another. See yourself delighting in your ability to unconditionally accept and understand this individual completely.

- In a relaxed state of honesty ask yourself—What do I appreciate about this person right now?

  For Example—Perhaps you appreciate the way that they smile, laugh, or the way that they help you when you really need it. Perhaps you have gratitude for the inner strength and courage that they possess. Perhaps you can appreciate the way that they treat, help, or love other people with whom they are close. Perhaps you can be grateful for the hidden ways in which they show their love for you.

- Now focus all of your attention on the feelings of gratitude for what it is that you do appreciate about this other person. Close your eyes and really allow yourself to feel divine reverence for another one of God's creations.

- Whenever you start to feel yourself focusing on the false lack, *immediately* replace that impression of limitation with the acknowledgment of that which you genuinely have high regard for about this person.

- Whenever you think about this person, think about the qualities that they have which are pleasing and genuinely good.

- When you have feelings about this person, experience feelings of sincere appreciation and fondness for the good qualities that they do have. Refuse, from this day forward, to be filled with emotions of a negative nature about anyone. Make your emotional atmosphere, in which you live all of the time, an atmosphere of unconditional love, eternal patience, divine forgiveness, and divinely-discerning understanding. Always allow all others to grow into their divine magnificence within your own emotional atmosphere. Embrace the opportunity to celebrate the divine nature of every soul.

- When you talk to others, talk about that for which you are grateful about this person. When you talk to others about this person, tell them about the divine potential for perfection that this person has within themselves. Let others help you to heal your relationship with this other person by filling their creative consciousness with the God-ordained vision of perfection that God has of this person.

FOURTH HEALING EXERCISE

- In a relaxed state of honesty ask yourself—What do I find myself complaining about, regarding my work, most of the time? *Perhaps you find yourself complaining about the hours, the atmosphere of the work environment, the duties that you need to perform.*

- Take this area of complaint and stop giving attention to it.

- Purposely refuse to think about this false complaint.

- Absolutely refuse to have any panic, displeasure, or failure feelings about this false complaint anymore.

- Decline to speak with others about this false complaint.

Now Visualize—how you would be living out your everyday work experience being absolutely free from all complaints. Feel yourself being enthusiastic about the day that is before you. Visualize yourself doing the work that you do with an inner attitude of appreciation for the opportunity to express the best that is within you!

- In a relaxed state of honesty ask yourself—What do I appreciate about my work right now?

    For Example*—Perhaps you are grateful for the pay that you receive. You really appreciate the people with whom you work. You enjoy the atmosphere in which you work. You like the hours that you are working. You look forward to a certain project with which you are working. Or you may appreciate the potential for advancement that you see in the future. You recognize the specific areas of training that you are learning which you can use in a future business that you want to start for yourself, where you are your own boss!*

- Now focus all of your attention on experiencing appreciativeness for what you *do love* about your work. Close your eyes and really allow yourself to experience passionate appreciation for that which you love to do.

- Whenever you start to sense that you are beginning to focus on a complaint, *instantaneously* replace the mental and emotional image of limitation about your work by intentionally experiencing passionate excitement about the intrinsic value of the work that you are doing.

- When you contemplate your work, think about those things from which you derive joy. Have appreciation for this opportunity to learn to rise about all negative thinking once and for all! Learn to think as one who is filled with the positive manifestation-power of appreciation in all that you do, all of the time.

- When you experience feelings about your work, let them be the feelings of excitement for the work that you are doing. Really feel appreciation for this opportunity to do all that you do for the Glory of God. Dedicate all that you do to the magnificence of the living Presence of God's Perfection expressing through you.

- Speak to others about how extraordinarily delighted you are about your work. With each word that you utter, voice words of appreciation about the chance that you have to put your best foot forward in all that you do. Whatever your work, speak to others about your work as if this were the most important work in the world for you or anyone else to do, for it may very well be so. We seldom see the greater vision that God has for our life and for ourselves, but we can be assured that at this time, and from day to day, if we are in a continual state of appreciation, we will always be guided to our rightful and most useful way to express our divine talents.

Study note: Work with the above exercises until you are completely healed of all that seems to stand in your way of living a life of appreciation. This work is extremely important, for what mostly stands in our way of fulfillment is the restrictive and repulsing attitude of criticism. When we heal all inner criticism, we are free to enjoy the expressions of appreciation. When we live the expressions of appreciation, we are open to receiving more of the infinite good that God has in store for us! Also work with the above exercises whenever you find yourself falling into the false habit of criticism in the future.

Most importantly of all, have fun with this lesson of study! Look forward to the freedom that you will have when you are healed of all negative thinking. Think about how wonderful you will feel when you are able to look at all areas of your life in an appreciative manner! Anticipate the creative manifestation-power for good that God's Presence, working through your creative feeling nature of appreciation, will be able to accomplish in your everyday life experience!

HEALING MEDITATION

- I take this sacred time to enter into the center of my heart, and here I freely allow myself to experience the unlimited, universal, and unconditional love that God has for me. As I rest within this healing love, I am assured that I am always one with the Presence of God. I allow the healing love of God to heal all within my mind and within my emotions that stands in the way of my really knowing God's Presence fully. I take a few minutes to rest in God's healing love. I take a few minutes to allow divine healing to take place within my mind and emotions.

- Now, as I rest within my heart center in a pure and peaceful state, I intentionally feel the unconditional love that God has for me radiating within my heart. I feel the Sacred Heart of God beating within my heart center. With every beat of my heart I realize that it is now the Sacred Heart of God that is beating my true life force and essence throughout my whole being and body. It is the sacred love of God that is now literally living through me. I completely accept this all-encompassing sacred-heart love into my being and into my life. I am rejuvenated by this all-encompassing sacred-heart love. I am healed of all that needs healing within this all-encompassing sacred-heart love. I am one with this all-encompassing sacred-heart love, and this all-encompassing sacred-heart love is a part of who I am.

- I fully allow my mental and emotional consciousness to expand with God's love. I literally radiate with God's love. I am an instrument for God's love to express through. I am the living demonstration of one who is the embodiment of God's love made manifest in human form.

- Accepting that I am an instrument for God's healing love to express through. I now bring to mind any area of my life that seems less than perfect, and I now send forth the healing transformative power of God's love expressing through me to surround and perfectly heal this area of my life, *and it is healed*, and will be made right and perfect through the power of God's All-Knowing wisdom.

- I affirm that the healing power of God's unconditional love living through me is the means through which my life and the lives of my loved ones are perfected and made whole. I give thanks to the Heart of God Who created me, my loved ones, and this life, so that I and all others can have the magnificent opportunity to be the living expressions of the living God in all of God's glory, beauty, dignity and majesty.

And So It Is.

4

Holistic Health—Getting Down to Basics

Author's note: The following lesson has been personally worked with and divinely interpreted from the truth of the teachings of Christ, which reveal the following realities of our Divine Selfhood.

What benefit is it if you gain the material fruits of this world through stress, worry, and strife, if you forfeit the joy and aliveness of the expression of your Soul in the process?

Through your personal expression of unconditional love for yourself as made in the image and likeness of God, and for your life as God's great gift to you, you are loving God with your whole heart, mind, and Soul, which is the first commandment of Christ.

Your Soul and body are kept perfect and free of all discord, through the expression of God living through you.

Getting down to basics concerning your health, this is an issue that is in the forefront of earthly living at this time. We, as a society, have great concern about the cost of health care, and we also have great concern about the quality of health care that is available to us at this time. The positive outcome of all of this worry and concern about our health care is that we are faced with the need for serious and concentrated focus on the *inner life* of the spiritual health of the *Soul*—which results in the outer health of the body. Health involves the health of our bodies, the health of our minds, the health of our emotions, and the most important health of all—the health of our Souls.

- Our Soul is the embodiment of the emotions and the experiences of all the life experiences that we have ever lived and will live in the future.

- Our Soul is the very fabric of subtle energies that make up all that we are. These energies make up our bodies, our lives, our personalities, and the health of all of the above.

If we are out of alignment and out of balance; if we are not feeling well in the sense of who we are as Perfect Spiritual Beings, and what our relationship is with the Presence of God at the center of ourselves; or, if our relationship with others is out of balance, then how can we expect to have a well-functioning physical body? How can we expect to have health and wholeness if the true mental-spiritual vehicle of our Soul, which is our well-spring of life, is out of order?

To bring balance and alignment to the body involves the use of positive mental thought and spiritual practices. In this lesson we will look at how the Soul is used as an energy field to bring a feeling of oneness between the Soul, God, our body, and our life.

SPIRITUAL DEFINITION OF THE SOUL

To fully understand the process that is involved in bringing balance and healing to our Soul—the true inner reality of who we are—it is helpful to contemplate the spiritual meaning and definition of the Soul.

- Throughout the major religious and philosophical thought systems of the world down through the ages, enlightened individuals have intuitively perceived that each human being has an important aspect to themselves that constitutes the core of who they are. This core, center, or spiritual reality of each individual is the true and absolute foundation of their divine personality, which is called the Soul. The Soul, the foundation of the pure, harmless, fearless, and unconditionally-loving personality of everyone is invisible to the human eye.

- Spiritually, the Soul is perceived as that element within all persons which is the supreme divine consciousness, the personal conscience behind the thoughts, emotions, and actions that constitute one's ability to choose right over wrong. The Soul is the divine, wise parent that exists within everyone, and this all-loving parent is the source of all pure and harmless behavior. The Soul is the truth of our divinely-perfect nature.

- The Soul is the eternal, immortal aspect of all human beings. The Soul is the invisible, though ever available, Presence of God, a literal personification of

God, the eternal life-force of the divine within us all. The eternal Soul of each individual eternally lives in the eternal Heart and Consciousness of God. The eternal Soul within each of us will reunite fully and consciously with the eternal Soul of God when our visible body has finished its earthly work and purpose.

Within this lesson we will be working on bringing healing and balance to our own limited and faulty recognition of the true reality of our Soul. We will be working on letting go of the negative thoughts and emotions, which constitute our imperfect human recognition of our Soul. Humanly, we tend to cover up the glory of our Soul through the acceptance of, and our own indulgence in, all kinds of thoughts, emotions, and actions of a negative nature which, in turn, create a lack of health on all levels of our emotional, physical, and intellectual lives. Within the following divinely perceived exercises, we will work on having purity and clarity of thought and emotion, and in so doing, we will find ourselves in a divinely-illumined state from which we will have a pure and unobstructed recognition of our immaculate Soul! From this recognition of our True Soul Reality we will seek to realize and to claim our natural state of unhindered health.

- Healing, and/or greater healing of the body, comes about when the free expression of the positiveness, the joy, the reality of the inherently pure goodness of your Soul is allowed to come forth and be expressed without any restrictions.

- Restrictions to our Soul's ability to freely express its divine magnificence originates from the negative personal ego—the part of us that feels that it is less than perfect, is highly critical and judgmental of others, ourselves, and of life as not being good enough. All of this negativity, and all of the problems that we have in this life are due to the false belief that we are separated from the unconditional love and power of God.

- We heal these internal energies of negativity and restriction by intentionally focusing on, becoming aware of, and allowing ourselves to freely permit our Soul—our divine nature of goodness—to express through us fully and completely!

GUIDELINES TO HEALING THE HEALTH OF YOUR SOUL WHICH WILL IN TURN BRING HEALTH TO YOUR BODY

- The law of the universe is one of continual inter-relatedness and interaction between all the energies that make up the mind of man and the Mind of God. You are influenced by all of these different energies of the mind. Whether they are positive or negative—they do have an effect on you.

- The energies of the negative human mind have power only when you are open to them by being out of alignment yourself. As you intentionally bring yourself into harmony with the energy, the Mind, and Soul of God—then are you in a position to personally function on this earth with all of your physical faculties in order. You are brought into harmony with the healing energy of God by the art and practice of meditation.

MEDITATION EXERCISE

Use this meditation every morning and evening for twenty minutes, for seven days, a month, or for however long you feel that you need to do so for complete and lasting healing. It would also be extremely helpful to you for your continual spiritual growth and continued health to repeat this lesson from time to time throughout the years ahead of you. Please be aware that each one of these spiritual lessons is designed in such a way that they will be able to bring you to a higher level of spiritual awareness each time that you really study them and earnestly put them into daily use.

Within this meditation exercise, you will bring your body, mind, and Soul into a state of inner alignment with the Soul of God. To do this, you will be repeating a Statement of Spiritual Truth to yourself that, in time, will fill your consciousness with the divine reality, which this statement of truth represents. The following statement of truth that you will be working with is spiritually designed to allow your Soul its unencumbered free expression of great joy and life abundant.

- As you center your thoughts on the rhythmic breathing of your breath, feel an inner letting go of the emotions, the vibrations, and the thoughts that are causing any sense of disharmony.

- As you center your feeling nature at the center of your heart, allow your heart to expand with *unconditional love* for the life that you are now living.

- As you rest deeper within the calm center of your heart, have an inner feeling of an inner cleansing and letting go *completely* of any and all negativity and stress.

- Now silently, slowly, repeatedly, say the following Statement of Spiritual Truth to yourself—

My Life Is A Great Joy To Live

As you repeat this grand truth to yourself, you will find that an immense volume of feeling for the preciousness and majestic quality of your life will start to surface. You will begin to fully allow your Soul to express its sincere feelings for the sacredness of the life that you are living. You will find that you are filled with an inner feeling of extreme excitement for the divine possibilities that your life now has, to be an instrument through which the truth of God can be expressed. Rest within the expansive energy of the eternal life and joy that your Soul desires to express.

> *Now continue onto the next level of this meditation exercise which will allow you to feel the energy of the Presence of God expressing throughout your entire being as the healing and balancing energy of warmth, the warmth of the truth of God revealed and expressed through your Soul. This feeling of warmth is experienced because you have allowed your Soul to fully and freely express its joy of being alive, without restraint or restriction from any form of negativity.*

As You Slowly and Silently Say to Yourself (Repeatedly) "My Life is a Great Joy to Live"

- Feel a warm glow within your body. This warmth represents the Healing Presence of God expressing through the vehicle of your Soul as your Soul freely expresses its great joy for living. The warm glow or feeling may feel intense—but comforting and healing. Rest in the inner glow, rest in the inner warmth for a comfortable amount of time.

- Surrender yourself, your body, your life, your thoughts, and your emotions to the healing glow of warmth of the wisdom and love of God in the center of your consciousness, in the center of your heart—to bring about the complete healing of the vehicle of your Soul.

Remember, your Soul is the vehicle through which God expresses the truth of God's Self. When your Soul is held back or shut down because of your personal indulgence in mental and emotional negativity, you need only to go within and become sensitive to your God-Center and the warmth of God's Healing Presence will dissolve the false negativity of your human personality so that your Soul is free to express the joy that it desires to manifest.

- Know that this inner warmth is the Healing Presence of God—aligning your physical body, your thinking process, and your emotional system with the Healing Truth of your Soul, of your divine reality.

- You may feel a change in your emotions or a change in your thinking. You may know a different way of living that is now better for you. Perhaps you are now more aware of how important it is for you to be in the Healing Presence of God more often. Perhaps you now realize how important it is for you to really relax within the Presence of the God that you are, in spiritual reality, at one with.

- Be aware and open to any guidance or change that comes to your attention as you rest in the warm glow of spiritual healing.

- When you feel refreshed, open your eyes and return to your outer activity to which you are now guided.

Balance of the Soul, the mind, the emotions, and your lifestyle is of extreme importance when it comes to the living of a life that is filled with health. When you ignore the health, balance, and well-being of any of the complexities that make up the Self that you are—then that imbalance of energy or vibration can have a negative effect on your body.

- **Added Exercise**—Silently repeat the statement of truth—*"My Life Is A Great Joy To Live"*—to yourself throughout the day and allow your heart and Soul to expand to even further heights of real joy! Repeat this statement of truth to yourself as you go about your day driving, shopping, working, interacting with others, etc., all day long, and see how aware you will become of the real joy that your Soul is really wishing to express through you as you live your everyday life. Keep in mind, that as you allow your Soul to freely express its great joy for living, you will be bringing a greater condition of health to your emotions, mind, and body!

CONTEMPLATION EXERCISE

To Think About and Use for Seven Days a Week, a Month, and Periodically Throughout Your Body

- Look at your life with an inner awareness of honesty and ask yourself—Is my life completely in balance with the Soul-Vibration that makes up the uniqueness of who I am?

If you are completely honest and if you truly desire to know—then it will be easy for you to sense where your outer lifestyle is out of balance with the inner Soul reality of who you are. You will sense an uneasiness about a certain area of your life, or you will feel unsure about a certain activity that you engage in, or you may feel uneasy about the quality of a relationship that you have.

All feelings of being unsure of yourself, and all feelings of disharmony can be vital clues to you, which can lead you to the answers you are seeking as to that which will bring you to the perfect health of your Soul.

The knowledge that you gain through the use of the meditation that is in this lesson will fill you with the inner guidance that is necessary for you to make the needed changes in yourself and in your lifestyle, which will be highly beneficial to you.

DAILY EXERCISES

To use and work with for seven days, a week, a month, or however long you need. Strive during this time of study to live an inner sense of balance, harmony, peace, beauty, and love.

EXERCISE ONE

Live in a continual state of balance within your mind, thoughts, emotions, and spirit. *Balance is the Inner State* of awareness that lets you express all aspects of your nature in a safe and successful way.

Give time to yourself, each day, to really listen to your inner intellect, inner thoughts, inner emotions, and the inner voice of your spirit. Make sure that you honor each important aspect of yourself by giving your undivided, unconditional, accepting attention to who you really are on a divine level.

- Be balanced in your daily positive expression of your intellect, your thoughts, your emotions, and your spiritual self. Let those that are close to you know what is expressing through you, on a positive level, throughout your entire being. Many times one may become unbalanced just because an important aspect of one's self is being neglected. Giving validation to your whole self is achieved when you safely share all that you are with those in your life who truly love and accept who you are.

- Take quiet time to look within yourself and define to yourself the aspects of your intelligence, your emotions, and your beliefs that you feel very good about. Take time to honor the good that is within you.

- Each of us has a balance of positive emotions, positive thoughts, and positive beliefs which need to be expressed so that we can truly be who we really are as a perfect Soul expressing through this human body.

  For Example—*There are times when we need to outwardly express our aliveness and joy in living. There are times when we need to outwardly express the thoughtful and intellectual side of our nature. There are times when we need to believe in, and outwardly express and vocalize, a higher ideal about life and living. There are times when we need to express outwardly our own feelings of sensitivity, compassion, and understanding of another person's life journey.*

- It will be highly advantageous to you to find a core group of personal friends where you feel safe in expressing who you really are. Find others who are of like mind and who are as loving, supportive, and accepting of you as you are of them. Have a group of friends who make up a "spiritualized mutual admiration society."

EXERCISE TWO

Live daily with a continual sense of harmony within yourself and in your relationships. *Harmony is the inner state* of unity, inner satisfaction, and positive acceptance of ourselves, others, and our environment.

• Concentrate on feeling complete harmony within yourself during the entire day and night. The vibrations of disharmony can easily cause one to be out of harmony physically, emotionally, mentally, and spiritually. Make a commitment to being harmonious on all levels of your being, regardless of how others are acting and regardless of disharmonious situations that may come your way.

• Decide in the morning that your inner and outer state of harmony is the harmony of your body. Decide that your inner and outer state of health is more important than any upset that you may encounter during the day. In proportion to your ability to stay harmonious within yourself, you will be bringing about inner vibrations of health and healing. So many diseases today are caused by daily stress and emotional upset. When you learn to counteract the negative influences of disharmony by refusing to be out of harmony—then you will know an inner strength that will protect you from any of the damaging influences of emotional unrest.

• Decide also, that you will feel only harmony within yourself when you are with others. Again, your health is more important than any argument or upset that you may feel or engage in with another. In the morning, decide that your mental health is going to harmonize all interactions throughout the day with everyone with whom you deal, live, love, and interact.

EXERCISE THREE

Live the continual feelings of peace in all of your activities. *Inner peace is felt* through the process of gratitude for all that you do have.

• The inner feeling and vibration of a peaceful countenance is a mighty tool for healing. As you go throughout your day, be keenly aware of any time that you feel less than peaceful. Instantly acknowledge the reason for the unrest. Usually this inner feeling of unrest, dissatisfaction, or frustration is easily healed by finding something for which to be grateful.

For Example—Once in a while when I am cleaning, I see the damage done by the last earthquake that we had in Los Angeles, and I sense an inner vibration of unrest. I instantly heal the negative vibrations of that unrest by firmly acknowledging my gratitude for being safely brought through that disruptive earth-shaking time.

• Whenever you feel unrest within yourself, train yourself to counteract the negativity of your thoughts and emotions by intentionally feeling the healing feeling of gratitude. You can always find something to be grateful for that pertains to the object or subject of the dissatisfaction.

EXERCISE FOUR

Live in a daily state of the conscious awareness of beauty. Be aware of the beauty of yourself and the beauty of life. *The healing energy* of acknowledged beauty brings joy to the mind—thus beauty becomes a real part of our body temple.

• Go through your day acknowledging the beauty that you express through your body, mind, emotions, and soul. In every thought that you have of yourself—feel and acknowledge how very beautiful you are. Let your body, thoughts, and emotions virtually vibrate with beauty.

• Whenever you come face to face with another, let yourself vibrate with the healing energy of beauty by acknowledging the other's **Inner Soul** beauty. Everyone is beautiful in their own special way, but we will not be able to enjoy it and benefit from it if we are too unaware to notice the beauty that is in our presence.

• Let the healing energy of beauty filter into your consciousness from your environment. Be aware of the beauty that is around you in nature or in the colors of the rooms that you are in; feel the beauty of the furniture that surrounds you, etc. As you let the concept of beauty filter into your awareness, you will benefit greatly from the healing effects of all that is around you for the enrichment, beauty, and enjoyment of your Soul. In proportion to your ability to be aware of the beauty that surrounds you—you become this beauty and your body is beautified in return.

EXERCISE FIVE

Live each day as an expression of love—be loving to everyone this week. *Love is the most powerful of emotions that helps to bring healing to us.*

- If you really want to benefit from love—dedicate yourself to completely and fully feeling and expressing love during the day. Refuse to let yourself indulge in the harmful feelings of hurt, anger, fear, or disappointment, for these negative emotions are the cause, or the potential cause, for serious physical problems.

- Whenever you feel unloved—take a moment, close your eyes and send unconditional love to yourself. Unconditionally love yourself the way that you would desire someone else to really love you.

- Whenever you think of someone else—send unconditional love to them in the same manner in which you would desire someone else to really love you.

- Whenever you find yourself in the presence of someone else, mentally close your eyes and send unconditional love to them in the same manner in which you would like to be unconditionally loved.

As you daily practice these spiritual exercises of spiritual balance and alignment, you will be well on your way to living a balanced life within your Soul, which will help to bring more balance and a greater sense of well-being to your body.

HEALING MEDITATION

- As I come into the quietness of my inner oneness with the Healing Presence of God—here I rest and let go completely of everything that may be a concern to me at this time.

- As I really let go of all negativity, I am brought into the inner healing vibration of God that now brings healing to my mind—my thoughts—my emotions—my body—and my Soul.

- In my oneness with God, I attain the cleansing of my Soul that results in inner and outer healing.

- Each time that I come to rest and commune with the Presence of God—my Soul is cleansed and brought into balance in whatever way is necessary for me to live a whole and productive life.

- I thank you Father-Mother God for the healing warmth of your love that now flows throughout my body and Soul. In your presence I am one with the glory that my Soul was meant to live.

And So It Is

5

You Are A Storehouse Of Spiritual Treasure

Author's note: The following lesson has been personally worked with and divinely interpreted from the truth of the teachings of Christ, which reveal the following realities of our Divine Selfhood.

My will is to do the perfect will of God.

My will is to do God's will by recognizing, accepting, cultivating, and showing forth the unlimited qualities and gifts of perfection that God has created me with in this lifetime.

My will is to show forth, to live, to demonstrate the perfect works of God.

My will, my life is to express the Light of God's perfection to the world around me.

"Come unto me, all of you who are unsure of who you are and wonder why you are here on earth, and I, God, the reality of your true-Self, will give to you the answer to all of your internal unrest and lack of confidence." (Jesus)

You are the very Light of God in expression; you are the very manifestation of the perfect nature and Soul of God expressing through your unique personality and physical form. You are the instrument through which the truth of God's unlimited magnificence is to be lived, shown forth, and demonstrated to the fullest. You are here on earth to bring forth and express the truth, beauty, and unlimited abundance of the Presence of God living through you within the life that you are now living.

You are here on earth to bring forth and express the truth, beauty, and unlimited abundance of God on all levels of your mind, emotions, and body. You are equipped to the fullest to bring forth the unlimited, All-knowing wisdom of God through the instrument of your mind and through the creative power of the rightful positive use of your daily thoughts. You are to show forth and express the perfect emotions of God that are always in a state of unconditional love, and spiritually-perceptive understanding of self, life, and others, exuberant joy, and eternal contentment. You are to bring forth the perfect nature of the Presence of God into the health of your body by knowing that the unconditional love of God has created your body and that the unconditional love of God sustains and maintains the perfect activity of your body at all times. Your body temple is also the holy instrument and vehicle through which the perfect presence and reality of God expresses forth to the fullest. You are the extraordinary manifestation of the physical existence of God in visible form.

You are also here on earth to bring forth, and express, the truth, beauty, and unlimited abundance of God in your relationships and careers. Within each of your relationships you are the vehicle through which God loves others unconditionally. Through the imaginative avenue of your career, it is the divine intelligence and the unlimited creativity of God that prospers you, your family, and the world around you. Each one of you, as the living representation of God in manifest form, is equipped, to the fullest extent, with the capability to bring fulfillment to every area of your life right *now*, just as you are!

Right here, within yourself, is an infinite and unlimited storehouse of special and unique personal talents that you were created to express to the fullest. Each one of these unique and spiritually-perfect talents was created within your consciousness from the perfect, unlimited Consciousness of God. All of these magnificent spiritual treasures that abide within your consciousness are waiting for you to put them into use. Your life is a life that is equipped with every quality, every talent, every insight, and every strength that you could ever imagine having the need of using in the life that you are now living. You were created to live this life, in which you find yourself, in a state of inner and outer prosperity of fulfillment in the areas of love, health, finances, and happiness.

WITHIN YOU IS A STOREHOUSE OF TALENTS EXERCISES

Following, are spiritual truths to work with, study, and use for a week, month, or for however long it takes for you to use this lesson to perfect your infinite storehouse of spiritual talents on a continual basis. Following each of these important spiritual principles are specific affirmations of truth that one should study and think about during the day. Take each affirmation of truth into a quiet and relaxed state of inner contemplation and, there, realize the truth of this affirmation as a part of your own self-reality. Take the truth of, the principle of, the spiritual reality of each affirmation into your daily everyday life experiences, and start to put these important spiritual truths and affirmations into daily practice. Only as these spiritual principles become a real part of yourself will your life start to change for the better.

SPIRITUAL PRINCIPLE ONE

You have a mind that is always connected to the grand-infinite-unlimited Mind of God. This Mind is always filled with the ideas that are necessary for you to use in your everyday life, which will bring to you prosperity and fulfillment.

AFFIRMATIONS

- My mind is one with the Ultimate Mind of the Universe and I am continually filled with Divine Ideas that lead me to my Ultimate Fulfillment.

- Every day I rest in the presence of Divine Wisdom, within my heart and mind, and I am continually filled with creative inspiration.

Daily exercise—Whenever you find that you need an answer, an idea, or a creative answer to a problem—take a few minutes to yourself, say the above affirmations to yourself in a quiet and reflective state of mind, and let the reality of their truth fill you with an inner sense of peace and confidence. Then as you return to your everyday activities, be on the alert to any intuitive answers, ideas, or feelings that come to your awareness. The divine wisdom of God is available to everyone who has the desire to listen (within) to the still small voice of God. It takes commitment, time, and practice to be a continually aware individual who is always attuned to the internal voice of God. So continue (consistently) to practice listening to the All-knowing divine wisdom of the Presence of God within your mind, every chance that you have to do so.

SPIRITUAL PRINCIPLE TWO

You have a heart that is connected to the Heart of God, and the Heart of God loves All without judgment or undue worry. When your heart is connected to the Heart of God—you are then *truly* a storehouse of unlimited, unconditional love that will fill you at all times with the love that you need to forgive and understand yourself, and all others that enter into your life experience. When you are freed from the negative emotions of hurt, anger, lack of self-esteem, aloneness, self-consciousness, and resentment—which all originate from an erroneous and restricted viewpoint of love—you have opened up the communication channel of God's higher wisdom to flow throughout your mind and heart. The unconditional love of God, flowing through you, is the source of communication between the divine wisdom of God and your human mind. When your heart is closed off to unconditional love, for any reason, you have closed off your inner communication with the Heart of God.

AFFIRMATIONS

- I am one with the Heart of God, which fills me continually with the Unconditional Love of the Universe, which created All That Is.

- My heart is beating with the rhythm of the Universal Heart of God and I am at peace."

Daily Exercise—Whenever you meet anyone: take a deep breath and affirm the above affirmations to yourself within the quietness of your mind and within the openness of your heart. Realize that, with the meeting of this other dear soul, you are in the sacred position of extending, on a verbal and nonverbal level, the universal Heart and Love of God expressing through you to the other soul. In proportion to your consistent ability to extend the universal Heart Love of God to another, you are healing any negative blockages that may be within any area of your psyche that is keeping you from having a clear communication with the Mind and Heart of God's Presence within yourself.

Spiritual Principle Three

You have unlimited strength that fills your body, mind, and emotions with a sureness and an inner peace that nothing of this world can take from you.

Affirmations

- In my union with God—my thoughts, my emotions, and my body are strengthened with the energizing power of the Universe.

- God continually guides me in all of my ways, which fills me with an inner sense of strength and sureness.

Daily Exercise—Your true source of inner and outer strength comes from the conscious awareness that knows that it is not the limited, human you, that does the doing; but rather, it is the Presence of God working through you that does the doing. Then all of your doings will be filled with unlimited strength, unlimited wisdom, and unlimited confidence. Whenever you find yourself thinking that that which you are doing is up to you to do, close your eyes for a moment and remember, acknowledge, and really feel that it is the Presence of God that is doing the doing, thus knowing that that doingness is perfect and unlimited.

Spiritual Principle Four

You have a body that is equipped to see you through the necessary means of self-expression that you need to fulfill your divine purpose here on earth. It is extremely important that you hold, and continue to hold, a conscious awareness of the spiritual reality of your body. For it is the mistaken materialistic belief about your body that allows it to become tired, old, and diseased. Thus, the following affirmations are extremely important for you to use and work with each and every day!

Affirmations

- My body is made up of the creative Love-Substance of God and I am whole, perfect, and energetic in all of my ways.

- I am the perfect embodiment of the Divine Activity of God.

- With every step that I take, I realize that it is God that is working through me to keep my body well and strong.

- I have a body, which is the perfect form for the fulfillment of the Divine Plan of God to express through.

- My material body is, in spiritual reality, the Spiritualized Perfection of God made manifest in all of its glory and splendor.

Daily Exercises—Start to change your perception of your body as being just a material housing for your Soul, to the real and elevated realization that knows that—*My body Is the spiritualized perfection of God made manifest.*

BEING ALL THAT YOU CAN BE

Following, is an exercise to practice each day for a week, month, or however long you choose. With the practice of the following exercise, you will come to recognize and develop your own personal storehouse of unlimited talents to the fullest. Realize each day that the Presence of God fills you to the fullest with all that you need to bring completion and fulfillment to the day before you. As you consciously bring into yourself the activity and power of God, then, and only then, are you using all the spiritual treasures that you were created with to the fullest extent possible.

EXERCISE

Whenever you think of a personal talent that you have need of that is necessary for your own sense of fulfillment—know within yourself that:

- In my oneness with the unlimited talents of God I already have___(fill in the blank with whatever the need is)__ within my consciousness just waiting to be expressed.

For Example—If you think that you need a greater personal sense of intelligence, affirm to yourself—In my Oneness with the unlimited talents of God I already have The Unlimited Intelligence of God's Mind within my consciousness just waiting to be expressed.

Exercise—Whenever you think of someone else or see someone else that embodies a personal talent that you have need of that is necessary for your own sense of fulfillment—know within yourself that:

• In my Oneness with the unlimited talents of God I already have__(fill in the blank with whatever talent another has that you perceive that you need) _within my consciousness just waiting to be expressed."

For Example—If during the day you see someone at work who exhibits a state of inner peace that you also desire to have, affirm to yourself—*In my oneness with the unlimited talents of God I already have The Eternal Peace of God within my consciousness just waiting to be expressed.*

Do the above exercises whenever you become aware that you have need of some talent that you feel that you are without. The emotional feeling of lack and unrest is a good indication that that talent is a talent, which you need to work on cultivating within yourself. As you fill in the above affirmations, take the emotional essence of the talent that you are working on cultivating and meditate on the reality of the essence of the talent within yourself, for as long and as often as possible.

For Example—If you feel that you are without the talent of expressing your best self freely (meaning that you feel that you are shy), know within yourself that:

• In my Oneness with the unlimited talents of God I already have an alive, enthusiastic, unhindered, eloquent nature within my consciousness just waiting to be expressed.

Within a meditative state, feel your oneness with the nature of God that always expresses a nature that is alive, enthusiastic, unhindered, and eloquent. Know that this very nature that you are seeking is already within you, waiting to be expressed. Now emotionally feel what it would be like to express the quality of enthusiasm when you speak to others, or when you work or play. Emotionally feel what it would be like to express the state of being eloquent in your speech, your actions, and your mannerism. At the conclusion of each meditation, commit yourself to putting these traits into action.

- Open yourself daily to the realization that you are ready to receive all of the unlimited talents and fulfillment that God and the universe have in store for you this day.

- Know that, because of your Oneness with the Presence of God, which always resides with your mind and heart, you are never limited in expressing any divine talents that you specifically have need of to be fulfilled in your life.

- Know that every talent that you have within yourself is a gift of love from God. As you express gratitude for the talents that you do have, in essence, you are preparing yourself to be in an open and receptive state to receive an even greater abundance of personal talents into your life. Use the talents that you are aware of having, *now* to the fullest, each and every day.

EXPRESSING YOUR DIVINE TALENTS EXERCISE

Following, are specific spiritual gifts for you to practice developing during the week, month, or however long you desire to work with this magnificent exercise. Each one of these spiritual gifts, when perfected, will bring a wealth of growth to your state of spiritual consciousness. Put into practice each divine talent or divine gift, one per day, each day of the week.

Each daily exercise will have three specific affirmations to say to yourself throughout the day. Each one of these affirmations is specifically created to bring to your conscious, everyday awareness, the spiritual truths and the spiritual treasures and gifts that are waiting within the consciousness of your soul to be expressed to a greater degree.

MONDAY

Express the divine talent, the divine gift of enthusiasm

Your gift is the Gift of Enthusiasm. The gift of enthusiasm is one of the most incredible gifts that you can give to others. For the gift of enthusiasm is also the gift of boundless energy and eternal expectancy for all-good to be demonstrated in your life and in the lives of all others. The energy of enthusiasm is also an extremely infectious emotion for others to emulate. Therefore, as you express enthusiasm within yourself you are also radiating this wonderful emotion to others that are around you, which they begin to express and multiply and this, in turn, will make your day even that much greater! Think how remarkable your day will be, being surrounded by highly enthusiastic people! And at the very least you will have an enthusiastic *you* to commune with throughout the day.

As you first awaken in the morning—think of how the day ahead of you is truly the day which God has made specially for you, thus it will be one of the most incredible days that you have yet to experience! Let yourself be in the continual atmosphere of divine enthusiasm for life. Allow yourself to consciously feel the Presence of God living this day through you. Let the atmosphere of your divine enthusiasm for life sweep up everyone else that comes into your day, into this majestic atmosphere of the reality of God—expressing as life, appearing to one and all—through your personal countenance of enthusiasm.

When you awaken in the morning say to yourself, silently or out loud, repeatedly, with feeling—

• This is going to be the most incredibly wonderful day of my life!

Periodically as you go through your day, regardless of any appearances to the contrary, say to yourself, silently or out loud, repeatedly, with feeling—

• This is indeed the most incredibly wonderful day of my life!

As you go to sleep at the end of your day, regardless of how your day may have appeared to be, say to yourself, silently or out loud, repeatedly, with feeling—

• This has been the most incredibly wonderful day of my life!

TUESDAY

Express the divine talent, the divine gift of the energy of Love

Your gift is the gift of Expressing Love. For everyone is in need of more quality love in their lives. Express love to everyone that you think about during the day, through the vehicle of your thoughts expressing through your open heart. Express love to everyone to whom you speak, whether in person or on the phone. Before you speak, feel the love of God within your heart and let that divine quality of love speak through you. Express love to every plant, flower, or living thing that you pass by. Realize that to some degree, every living thing has the life-force of God expressing through it. Express love to every animal that comes into your day. Let yourself, fully and completely, feel the freedom and joy of expressing unconditional love to everyone and everything in your life. Commit yourself to freely and continuously feeling more love this day than ever before!

When you awaken in the morning say to yourself, silently or out loud, repeatedly, with feeling—

• I am going to love more freely and fully, this day, than ever before!

Periodically as you go through your day, regardless of any appearances to the contrary, say to yourself, silently or out loud, repeatedly, with feeling—

• I am spiritually rejuvenated by God's love expressing through me, *now*!

As you go to sleep at the end of your day, regardless of how your day may have appeared to be, say to yourself, silently or out loud, repeatedly, with feeling—

• I am the most loving person that this world has ever seen!

WEDNESDAY

Express the divine talent, the divine gift of *Happiness*

Your special gift is a Gift of Happiness. Give your gift of happiness to the world around you, for this world is so in need of happiness. Keep in mind that the spiritually evolved soul is a soul who is freely happy the majority of the time. And the truth of the matter is that you are happy because you know who you are spiritually! When you know who you are spiritually, it is always a source of happiness and joy to extend that realization out to others. One who is spiritually illumined is one who is, or at least is striving to be, genuinely happy to be alive. For one who is illumined, is one who knows, or at least intuitively perceives, that the life that they are living is a precious gift from the Presence of God. Consequently, it is to your continual spiritual evolvement and to the evolvement of others, that you sincerely commit yourself to celebrating the life that you have, through the joyful expression of true and genuine happiness.

When you awaken in the morning say to yourself, silently or out loud, repeatedly, with feeling—

• I am extremely happy to be alive this day!

Periodically as you go through your day, regardless of any appearances to the contrary, say to yourself, silently or out loud, repeatedly, with feeling—

• I am increasingly happy to be alive this day!

As you go to sleep at the end of your day, regardless of how your day may have appeared to be, say to yourself, silently or out loud, repeatedly, with feeling—

• Each day my ability to be naturally happy increases immensely!

THURSDAY

Express the divine talent, the divine gift of *Seeing The Spiritual Truth*

Your gift is the gift of Seeing The Spiritual Truth. See the spiritual, positive truth in all situations that seem humanly negative. Give your talent of seeing the higher truth to others that are still unsure of whom they are spiritually. Bring to them the spiritual principle of God's All-goodness, everywhere present, in all situations, so that God's truth and God's Presence can work in their lives to make them whole and prosperous.

Take the truth that you have just studied within this lesson and put it into real practice. Whenever you see someone thinking negatively, or thinking and acting without wisdom during the day, realize that your mind is one with the All-knowing Mind of God, and that you are now thinking the true and right thoughts of God. Now proceed to express these true thoughts of God in the right way and at the right time to those that are in need of a clear mind. Whenever you perceive that someone is feeling negative feelings, instantly connect with the Heart of God and let the unconditional love of God flow through you, to guide you in how you can help another feel good about themselves again. Commit yourself to being a living example, a living demonstration of your special spiritual talents and gifts. A gift is only a true gift when it is taken out of its hiding place and freely and joyfully given away.

When you awaken in the morning say to yourself, silently or out loud, repeatedly, with feeling—

• I am the instrument through which God's truth heals all negativity!

Periodically as you go through your day, regardless of any appearances to the contrary, say to yourself, silently or out loud, repeatedly, with feeling—

• I am inspired by the truth of God flowing through my mind and heart!

As you go to sleep at the end of your day, regardless of how your day may have appeared to be, say to yourself, silently or out loud, repeatedly, with feeling—

- The truth of God flowing through my mind and heart is healing all untruth of the day just past!

FRIDAY

Express the divine talent, the divine gift of Inner Calmness

Your gift is the gift of Inner Calmness. Intentionally feel the inner calmness within yourself that knows, without a shadow of a doubt, that this day is completely controlled by the higher spiritual laws of God's divine order. Know that this day is being perfectly created out of the consciousness of God that knows only perfection.

Express calmness in the times of outer chaos in your day. Whenever events seem to be without divine order, become still within yourself, refuse to react, and bring the divine order of God into action through the vehicle of your inner calmness. Give your gift of calmness to others that seem to be in short supply of this special gift.

When you awaken in the morning say to yourself, silently or out loud, repeatedly, with feeling—

- This is the day, which God has created out of a creative consciousness of divine order!

Periodically as you go through your day, regardless of any appearances to the contrary, say to yourself, silently or out loud, repeatedly, with feeling—

- I am continually expressing the healing and creative power of inner divine calmness to the world around me!

As you go to sleep at the end of your day, regardless of how your day may have appeared to be, say to yourself, silently or out loud, repeatedly, with feeling—

- Peace be still and know that I am God.

SATURDAY

Express the divine talent, the divine gift of Appreciation

Your gift is the gift of Appreciation. When you express your gift of appreciation, you multiply whatever it is for which you are appreciative. This also is a wonderful gift to express to others that are in need of abundance in their own lives. If another is in a false state of lack, you can easily be an example to them of one who is demonstrating the multiplying power of appreciation through your abundant expression for appreciation of all good things that are in your life. Be in the habit of inwardly and outwardly saying "Thank you" whenever you appreciate something or someone.

As you go through your day, be aware of everything and everyone that you appreciate and multiply the essence of that person, circumstance, or object in your life through the abundant power of appreciation. Appreciate the air around you and multiply the essence of a joyous life. Appreciate the love that is within you and you multiply the essence of love in your life. Appreciate a smile that another gives you and you multiply the essence of loving kindness being expressed towards you.

When you awaken in the morning say to yourself, silently or out loud, repeatedly, with feeling—

- I commit myself to being aware of all that I appreciate this day!

Periodically as you go through your day, regardless of any appearances to the contrary, say to yourself, silently or out loud, repeatedly, with feeling—

- I multiply in my life the essence of everything that I appreciate this day!

As you go to sleep at the end of your day, regardless of how your day may have appeared to be, say to yourself, silently or out loud, repeatedly, with feeling—

- I fully appreciate the gift of the day just past, thus multiplying the essence of living a magnificent life!

SUNDAY

Express the divine talent, the divine gift of Union With God

Your gift is the gift of Union with God. When you feel the Presence of God within yourself during the day, you give the gift of God's Presence to all others that come into your conscious awareness.

As you go about your day feel that the Presence of God is with you all day long. Feel the Presence of God within yourself as an inner feeling of peace, love, joy, and contentment. As you remind yourself that the Presence of God is always with you, you will literally be one with the Presence of God through your conscious awareness of this fact. Remember that the Presence of God is always with you; all you need to do is to remind yourself that this is so.

When you awaken in the morning say to yourself, silently or out loud, repeatedly, with feeling—

- I am consciously one with the Presence of God!

Periodically as you go through your day, regardless of any appearances to the contrary, say to yourself, silently or out loud, repeatedly, with feeling—

- Wherever I go the Presence of God goes before me to make the less than perfect situations perfect!

As you go to sleep at the end of your day, regardless of how your day may have appeared to be, say to yourself, silently or out loud, repeatedly, with feeling—

- The Presence of God is becoming more noticeable and clear within my conscious awareness throughout the night!

Everyone has special talents and gifts right now—and as you use them, they will strengthen and open up the energy that is within you for the cultivation of new and better gifts of spiritual-self-expression.

6

Spiritualizing A Love Relationship

Author's note: The following lesson has been personally worked with and divinely interpreted from the truth of the teachings of Christ, which reveal the following realities of our Divine Selfhood.

When you consciously and sincerely love God with your whole heart, mind, and soul—you are filled with unconditional love.

When you continually love God with all of your heart and mind—you are then able to accept the unconditional love that God has for you.

When you love God with your whole heart, mind, and soul—you are then able to extend that same quality of unconditional love to others that are in your life.

When you love God with your whole heart and mind—and you know, without a doubt, that God loves you unconditionally—then you know that you are a divine instrument through which the Presence of God, loving through your heart, loves others unconditionally.

Love is the only real and lasting essence in your life that has any real value. Knowing how to really love someone spiritually is the only way to find true and lasting happiness in your life.

THIS LESSON CAN BE USED IN MANY WAYS

This lesson will be highly beneficial to you if—you have a special love relationship and you want to work on making it better, plus you want your present relationship to grow more fully. This lesson will be highly beneficial to you if—you are dating someone and you want to find out,

77

by using the following techniques for spiritualizing that relationship, if this relationship is really the right relationship for you. This lesson will be highly beneficial to you if—you want to draw the right love relationship to you. In this lesson you will find out how to work on your own inner "Spiritualized-Love-Capability." The qualities of love that you have within yourself will attract to you the qualities of love that are within another. The one that you attract is a mirror to you, reflecting back to you the person that you truly are within yourself. This lesson can also be extremely beneficial to you if—you are alone, for the work that you do on developing your own inner Spiritualized-Love-Capability will develop your own spiritual growth immensely. This lesson will be highly beneficial to you if—you want to have more love for yourself. You will find yourself loving who you really are more and more as you put into practice the art of developing spiritualized-love.

PRINCIPLES OF SPIRITUALIZED-LOVE

- Having spiritualized-love in your life and in your relationships is the only lasting kind of love that one can have. Spiritualizing the love that you have is the only way to keep a relationship strong and harmonious.

- When your love relationship is based upon human need, then that relationship is not really formed from spiritualized-love. Any relationship that is based on anything less than spiritualized-love is shallow and without any real substance! If you have a relationship that is not based on spiritualized-love, then it most likely will be based on physical attraction, financial need, or perhaps out of a sense of loneliness, which are all based on the false beliefs of this world and on the false beliefs of neediness and scarcity. Remember, for whatever *selfish or selfless* reason that you have chosen your relationship, that reason will be the main body of your experience within that relationship, for good or bad.

- To have real spiritualized-love within yourself you must take time daily to do the spiritual work that is necessary so that you are free from the fear of not being loved. Freedom from the fear of not being loved is gained from knowing that—because of your oneness with the Presence of God within your heart and mind—all of your needs are already taken care of by the unconditional love that God has for you.

- When you are free from the need to be loved and/or the need for someone else to take care of you, then you are ready to share real spiritualized-love with another, because you know that you are already whole and complete within yourself because of your oneness with the unconditional love of God, which always resides within your heart.

- When you are one with the unconditional love of God's Presence the majority of the time, then you are ready to share with another a life that is based on communicating the selfless, unconditional love of God expressing between the two of you.

TRAITS OF TRUE SPIRITUALIZED-LOVE

- True spiritualized-love is found within your selfless ability to release most or many of your personality needs so that you can put the best interests of your loved one before your own.

- Spiritualized-love is always found in your desire to encourage another's spiritual growth. Spiritualized-love is found within your ability to selflessly help another with their spiritual growth and study.

- Real spiritualized-love is found within your selfless ability to encourage another in attaining their highest dreams.

- Real spiritualized-love is found within your ability to be able to see the highest good in your loved one and keeping this high vision of them always before you.

- A true spiritual partnership and/or spiritual relationship is between equals. A spiritual partnership is based on the union of two souls who consciously seek to further their soul growth and spiritual evolution within the framework of that relationship, thus keeping that relationship spiritually alive and growing spiritually.

MEDITATION EXERCISE
TO USE FOR THE ENTIRE PERIOD OF STUDY

Meditate on your inner ability to love others unconditionally each day, for a week, a month, or for whatever length of time that you decide to work with this lesson, to obtain the realization of yourself as the Love of God in expression.

Each morning and evening during this week, month, or for the entire length of time that you choose to study this lesson; go for fifteen to thirty minutes into a peaceful, quiet, relaxed state of deep meditation and realize fully, completely, and freely that you are one with the unconditional, spiritualized-love of God.

For five to ten minutes, contemplate, accept, become one with, and realize that—

• *You* are the instrument through which the spiritualized-love of God is able to express to others.

For the next five to ten minutes, contemplate, accept, become one with, and realize that—

• *You* are unconditionally loved by God all of the time. Be at one with the unconditional love that God has for you. Rest in your oneness with the unconditional love of God.

For the final five to ten minutes, contemplate, accept, become one with, and realize that—

• The very love of God is filling you now, so that you can go out into your day to express this very same love to all others with whom you come into contact.

Visualization Exercise

At the end of your meditation—view yourself within your mind's eye. See the inner view of yourself, going out into the day before you, being filled with the unconditional love of God that is flowing out from you as an invisible energy-wave of love that enfolds everyone that you encounter. This energy-wave of love that is unconditionally flowing out from you to all others is blessing and uplifting everyone in the healing power of God's love. See yourself as being a blessing to all others. Change your concept of yourself from one who is self-centered to one that is freely giving from the pure, unconditional love that is from your purified heart and soul.

Exercises, Steps, and Affirmations

Following, are exercises, steps, and affirmations to use, for a week, month, or however long you need to work with them, which will guide you to the attainment and development of the necessary ingredients for having a spiritualized-love relationship with everyone. Each of the following exercises, steps, and affirmations should be focused on, studied, and put into practice each day of the week, month, or however long you are working with Spiritualizing your love capacity.

Morning Intent to Love Unconditionally

Affirmation—

- As I awaken in the morning I take a few minutes to intentionally open my heart up to the great Unconditional Love of God, which, in turn, connects me with all others on a heart-to-heart level.

When you first awaken in the morning you will find that this is the perfect time to open your heart to the day before you and commit yourself to being in the reality of God's unconditional love throughout the day.

Exercises—

- In the morning, and throughout the day, commit your day to intentionally connecting with all others on a *heart-to-heart* level of communicating unconditional love to and for them. Remember that unconditional love is a love that is given without conditions. It is a pure and thoughtful love that does not expect anything back in return. Communicate with all others from the deep level of your heart, where you sincerely wish for them their highest good on all levels of their being and in their life. Communicate to all others from the deep true level of your Soul-Self by sincerely working on really wanting to see and know the real loving and giving *Self* that you know is within the one with whom you are communicating. Communicate to all others from the deep true level of your Soul-Self by sincerely working on really wanting others to see and know the real loving and giving *You* that you are.

- As you awaken in the morning and throughout the day, commit yourself to giving real unconditional love and appreciation towards yourself. Be genuinely grateful for the loving self that you really are. Give yourself the freedom to express the unconditional love that is within your heart. Remember that you need not fear being hurt by others because you are loving them unconditionally and you are loving them without expecting anything in return, thus you cannot be hurt. Give real unconditional love and appreciation to all others. Do not hold back your appreciation and love for yourself and for others. The love and appreciation that you freely and unconditionally give to yourself and to others is filled with healing energy.

- As you awaken in the morning and throughout the day, really and freely know that the greatest love that you can have is in being who you really are, and knowing that you are unconditionally loved by God just the way you are. Realize fully that you have no need to change your true inner spiritual nature to have love in your life. Also realize that you have no need to change anyone else—you can love their real, true spiritual self just the way they are.

YOUR DIVINE PURPOSE AND MEANING IS TO EXPRESS LOVE

Affirmation—

- In my realized Oneness with GOD—I know that my true purpose in life is to be a perfect expression of Spiritualized-Love.

One of your divine purposes in this life is to be the expression of God's unconditional, spiritualized-love. Your divine purpose is to help the progress of the spiritual growth of others in whichever ways that you feel intuitively guided to do so by the Heart of God expressing through you. When you know that you are already filled with the unconditional love of God that is always fulfilling all of your needs, then you are able to stand back emotionally, meaning that you emotionally need nothing from another, and look to see what another is in need of so that they can grow strong and secure within themselves.

Exercises—

• During the day, whenever you find yourself in the presence of another, stand back within yourself emotionally, from a pure heart, needing nothing from them, and ask yourself how you can help this individual to feel more self-confident. Perhaps you will sense that they need to be complimented on something that they do well, or perhaps they need to hear about how much you appreciate the kind things that they do, and more.

• Whenever you find yourself in the presence of a friend or loved one, stand back within yourself emotionally, from a pure heart, needing nothing from them, and ask yourself how you can help this individual to feel hopeful about a problem that they have in their life. In a quiet and peaceful manner, from a sincere heart, ask them how their life is at this time and see what areas they are concerned about. Then say what you are guided to say to them, from your heart, that will give them hope and an inner feeling that somehow, some way, everything will work out fine.

• Endeavor to wish *only* unconditional happiness, goodness, and fulfillment for all those that you think about, speak to, and interact with this day. Live every moment of this day and every day wanting only the *best* for all others!

UNDERSTANDING THE HEART OF ANOTHER
MEDITATION OF THE HEART

Affirmation—

• I find myself in a true Spiritual Love Relationship of Oneness and Understanding—when in meditation I truly consider the other person's position by becoming the other person.

When you join your heart with the heart of another in meditation—you become *one* with them. When you join with another in your heart, you obtain a real sense of understanding of what their viewpoint is about themselves, their life, and of the situations that they are going through.

Exercise—

Whenever you need added understanding of one that you love, take a few minutes to practice the following meditation of the heart:

- Become still within yourself, put aside any personal sense of self-centeredness, hurt, or concern, etc., and intentionally desire to feel the unconditional love of God within your own heart. Rest within this inner state of divine love until you feel completely at peace.

- Now intentionally join your heart to the heart of the one that you love. Feel your divine oneness with them, with a sincere and pure desire to understand what is within their heart. Sincerely desire to understand and see their viewpoint about a problem, or about how they feel about an issue that is within their life, or desire to understand a fear that they have, and so on. Then you will be filled with the needed understanding of the other people that are in your life experience.

- At the conclusion of your heart-to-heart meditation, open yourself to the All-understanding nature of God—which will lead you to the right way to feel, the right words to say, and the right actions to take in all of your relationships so that healing is achieved through your divine understanding.

DEVELOP A DIVINELY TRUSTING NATURE

Affirmation—

- In the State of Oneness with Spiritualized-Love—I release all fear, worry and concern—and I trust the Guidance of God to make all things right.

Love is not enough in any relationship that you have. You must also work on developing a stronger and firmer level of Divine Trust in all of your current and future relationships. The energy of trust—builds trust.

Exercises—

- Work on your own ability to trust the one that you love which will build around you a powerful vibratory field of trust which, will then, bring trust into your life. If you are meditating daily and if you are turning to the divine guidance of God's Presence within your mind and heart on a consistent basis, you will know in your heart if someone is not a trustworthy person, and you will know that that relationship will not be a good one for you to become involved. But, if you intuitively feel that someone is worthy enough of trust for you to become involved with them, then it is far healthier for the relationship to trust them unconditionally. If at some point they prove themselves to be untrustworthy, then that will be the time to make new decisions about that relationship based on the divine guidance that you receive from God.

- If you are a trustworthy person—you will draw more trustworthy behavior to yourself in all areas of your life. Work on being a trustworthy person in your love relationships, and then you will draw to yourself others who love you, and who are trustworthy in that relationship.

- If you are already in a committed spiritualized-love relationship or if you are contemplating becoming involved in a committed spiritualized-love relationship, it is extremely important that you be free from any mistrustful feelings of jealousy, hurt, or fear. This is done by remembering that if you have a real spiritualized-love relationship between yourself and another, that another person cannot come into that relationship and take that love from you. If someone really loves you within a spiritualized, divine-love relationship, then another cannot enter into that relationship to take that person, or to take that love from you. But if someone does, then that person really did not love you unconditionally with the quality of spiritualized divine love that you are worthy of having. So bless them and release them, knowing that you deserve a spiritualized-love that no one can enter into to defile.

- Work on being a trustworthy person in your field of work, and your work will treat you in a trustworthy manner. Be one who is the kind and quality of person that you would hire to work for you.

- Work on being a trustworthy person as far as the words that come out of your mouth. Ask yourself if the words that you are speaking are equally truthful and kind. It is possible to tell that truth and still be kind in doing so.

GIVE A 100% COMMITMENT TO YOUR RELATIONSHIPS

Affirmation—

- Whenever God—The Universe—brings Spiritualized-Love into my life, I *commit* myself to the growth of that relationship, whether that relationship is with a loved one or a friend.

Exercises—

- In every relationship before you—give it your all, on all levels. *Give to each of your relationships your 100% all and commitment.*

- If you give your all to every relationship that you have and then one of them does not work out, at least you know that you did all that you could to make it work, and at the very least, you have grown and become a better person spiritually because of that relationship.

- Within each of your love relationships, freely and fearlessly give all of your heart; give all of your dreams and hopes; give all of the truth of your personal self, so that you know within yourself that you did all that you could to share with another the truth of who you are, the truth of the life that you desire to live, and the truth of your inner-most heart.

- Within each of your personal friendship relationships, risk—with those that you really trust intuitively—sharing most of your fears, your dreams and hopes, and the areas in which you would desire help to grow spiritually strong within yourself. Our personal relationships can be some of the greatest unconditionally-loving relationships that we will ever have, if we give them the time and the chance to grow and blossom. Unfortunately, many people put more worth and energy into their romantic relationships and let the real lasting relationships of friendship slide by. Many times a true friend is there when a romantic relationship has gone astray.

- If you focus on the success of your relationships instead of the possible failure, then your relationships have a much better chance of being great!

REALIZE THAT YOU ARE THE EXPRESSION OF GOD'S LOVE

Affirmation—

- My life is one of continual Spiritual Growth—I am here on earth to express Spiritual Love to the fullest—*And So It Is*.

Exercises—

- Every day—go out into your day, making a firm and absolute commitment to being the most loving person in the world—and then live your day of love to the fullest!

- Look at every person that comes into your day, as God would see them. God would see each person as God's beloved son or daughter in whom God was well pleased. Think of what a blessing of spiritualized-love you would be if you would see everyone within this same light of perfection. If you would see everyone that comes into your life through the eyes of God then you would be one of the greatest blessings that this world has ever seen. For as you know, we all are in need of someone special in our lives who sees the truth of who we are through the eyes of unconditional, spiritualized-love and just think, you can be that blessing in the lives of many.

- Really realize right now—and remind yourself during the day—that you are unconditional, spiritualized-love in expression, and because you are the love of God in human form—you are now living the life of the most blessed Soul on earth! *And So It Is!*

HEALING MEDITATION

- Divine Presence at the center of my heart—I come to you with the sincere desire to love the way that You love. I come to You with the yearning need to give to this world the love with which You are now filling my heart and Soul.

- I come to you Dear Presence—to offer my life to "living love" every day of my life to the fullest.

- I am the most blessed of your creations—for I now know the true meaning of love and I am complete today—tomorrow—and throughout eternity.

And So It Is

7

Mental, Emotional, Physical, Spiritual Balance Creates Perfect Health

Perfect Holistic Balance Creates Perfect Health
What to Do When You Are Feeling Under the Weather
Emotionally, Mentally, Spiritually, and Physically
How to Keep Yourself in Perfect Balance, Emotionally,
Mentally, Spiritually, and Physically All of the Time

Author's note: The following lesson has been personally worked with and divinely interpreted from the truth of the teachings of Christ, which reveal the following realities of our Divine Selfhood.

This day that I am living is the perfect day that God has created for me to live—within the mental, emotional, physical, and spiritually balancing and healing power of peace, joy, and inner and outer contentment and fulfillment.

I am filled with emotional and physical health in proportion to my ability to continually focus on the Presence of God within my heart and mind, which results in my being in an inner healing state of peace and stillness.

I will be filled with perfect health—mentally and physically—in proportion to my ability to be free of critical judgments; and to judge righteous judgment, which is based on God's divine wisdom flowing through my mind as my heart, is filled with loving kindness and spiritualized understanding.

Physician—one who is consciously one with the Presence of God within one's heart and mind—heal yourself!

W henever you are feeling a bit out of balance, emotionally, mentally, or physically—whenever you are beginning to feel a bit under the weather—that is the time to immediately turn within to find out what your body and soul are really trying to tell you; it is the time to immediately look at the areas within yourself that are without harmony. Look within yourself to see whether the disharmony is in any area of your body, your thoughts, or your emotions. Feeling under the weather, feeling less than whole and complete within yourself and within your life is a warning signal for you to look within.

In most cases, you will realize a state of disharmony first within the area of your emotional life before the physical body shows the outer signs of inner emotional stress and imbalance. These emotional warning signs can embody the feelings of just being out of it; or feeling tired, feeling unhappy, worried or hopeless, which then may lead to the physical warning signs of pain, hurt, sniffles, a cold, or flu.

When any of these warning signs present themselves to you, that is the time to:

- Take more time to yourself.

- Look into the inner reason for your discomfort.

- Look inside yourself and see where you need to make improvements.

- Maybe you need more time for yourself.

- Perhaps your diet needs change.

- Maybe you need to be living a lifestyle that is without as much stress.

- Perhaps your life just needs to have more real meaning.

- Do you need to change the quality of your friendships so that they are more positive and supportive?

- Does your over-all basic lifestyle need changing?

- Perhaps you need to ask yourself if you are really living the dreams that you hold dear to your heart so that your everyday life has more meaning and fulfillment.

The exciting and healing truth is that you have within yourself the natural capability to achieve well-being. You have at your fingertips the positive and healing Presence of God within your mind (thoughts) and heart (emotions). God's All-wisdom is always available to you to turn to for the answers that you are seeking.

When Your Body is Off Balance

Look at the areas within yourself and within your life where you feel that you are out of balance or out of sync with your personal relationship with the Presence of God within your mind and heart, with your personal God-Self-Reality, with your physical body, with your emotions, with your work, and with your relationships. *For these are all clues to where more balance is needed.*

SEVEN STEPS AND AFFIRMATIONS

Following, are basic steps to follow whenever you are feeling a bit out of balance emotionally, mentally, or physically—whenever you feel under the weather emotionally and/or physically. The following steps and affirmations are also beneficial in bringing about the clarity and balance within your whole being, which is needed so that continual health is the norm in your life.

Study each of the following steps and affirmations daily for a week, a month, or however long it takes to attain a feeling of over-all health and well-being. Take each affirmation, which represents a spiritual principle of truth, into your daily meditation, feel the spiritual reality of that spiritual truth, and let it filter throughout your entire being. Work with these affirmations and steps during the day to achieve the ultimate level of health possible—emotionally, physically, and spiritually.

FIRST STEP
TAKE TIME TO HEAL YOUR EMOTIONAL BODY

Affirmation—Spiritual Principles of Truth

- I bring healing, *balance, and alignment* to my emotions by letting go of all criticism, judgment, and dissatisfaction which, in turn, brings the healing vibrations of inner peace, contentment, and harmony to my body for healing, wholeness, and rejuvenation.

Daily Exercises—

Our emotions affect our body for good or bad, so it is of great importance to intensely look at your emotions and see where you are out of balance.

See if there is any area within your thoughts and your emotions where you are being overly critical of yourself—of others—and of your life, and *list below*. Being overly critical will bring about the restrictive feelings of resentment, irritability, animosity, anger, upset, exasperation, annoyance, and emotional and physical stress.

• _

• _

• _

• _

Take a moment of inner *contemplative silence* with each criticism that you have just listed above. In the inner silence, realize completely that the criticism that you have about yourself, about another, or about your life is just your personal inner sense of disquiet and uneasiness about a false picture, or false image, that you hold within your mind about yourself, another, or your life—is somehow being less than perfect. Realize that this physically, emotionally, and spiritually-disruptive sense of being *highly critical* has now come to your attention to be healed and released through the knowingness of the spiritual truth which will set you free from the disruptive emotional energies of being critical; which then, will give you freedom from added stress to your emotions, mind, spirit, and body.

The healing truths that will set you free from the harmful feelings of being critical are as follows—

• You, all others, and all of life are made in, and out of, the perfect image and likeness of God.

• Within the Consciousness of God, within the Mind of God, there is a perfect image of yourself, all others, and of life, from which all that is created.

- All that you perceive as the entire universe is created out of, and contained within, the Consciousness of God. The creative Consciousness of God is the one and only source of all that is. The Consciousness of God is only aware of infinite and unlimited perfection.

Realize that that of which you are critical is not a reality within the Consciousness of God—Who knows only perfection. Remember that you and all others are made in the perfect image and likeness of God, whether or not one realizes this truthfully and whether or not one expresses this truthfully. Remember that your life is the life that God has made for you to rejoice in and you need to be content and fully satisfied. Whatever you are being critical of is just a false sense of yourself, another, or your life that needs to be healed. Let go of and heal all criticism by intentionally elevating your personal, *perhaps limited* state of consciousness to the level of God's Consciousness of perfection. God-Consciousness is the awareness of perfection within yourself, within others, and within life. Know that within the Consciousness of God this so-called source of irritation will be healed some way, somehow, in the right way and at the right time. Being in the energy of criticism will not heal the source of the criticism; it will only make it more pronounced, thus agitating your mind, emotions, and body to an even greater extent!

If you are being critical of yourself—decide to change what you are able to and let go of the criticism. For example—You feel that you are too critical. So you inwardly realize that the true image of the real you which is always held within the Consciousness of God; is an image of one who is never critical, one who is always satisfied, content, and fulfilled from within themselves. Then decide to release any feelings of being critical in the future, knowing that that feeling is not a part of your real God-Self-Nature.

If you feel highly critical of another—know that within the Consciousness of God, the trait exhibited by another that bothers you, does not exist. Know that this disagreeable trait that another has is only brought about through their ignorance of who they are as being made in the perfect image and likeness of God. Through your knowingness of their true perfection, even though it may be deeply hidden within their nature, you may help to heal them of what it is that annoys you. But, most importantly of all, you will personally be free of those disruptive feelings of criticism!

If there is an area or aspect of your life with which you are highly critical, know that what you accept or what you focus on with great emotion tends to be recreated in the same image of perceived imperfection. So it is best, for healing of the problem and for the overall healing of yourself, to join with the perfect picture that the Consciousness of God has for your life. Know that within the Consciousness of God the perfect plan for your life has already been created. Inwardly trust that the unconditional love that God has for you will guide you to harmonious life experiences. All you need do is to let go of the negative vibrational emotions of being critical, which hold you in bondage to the false picture of imperfection, and trust that God will guide you to your perfect style of living in the right way and in the right time.

As you let go of all that causes you to feel critical, you not only heal what seems to be less than perfect, but most importantly, you release the negative emotions of being critical from your body so that you can come into a more harmonious state of health.

See if you are feeling and thinking thoughts of negative judgment, of not being good enough, about yourself and *list below*. These thoughts and feelings of not being good enough can easily bring about the false emotions of shame, self-contempt, hopelessness, and holding oneself back from showing forth the perfection of God's Presence living through them, as them. Being in the false energy of, not being good enough, can bring about immense and needless stress within the entire psyche and physical body; for the false feelings and thoughts of not being good enough go completely against the truth of who you are spiritually!

• _

• _

• _

• _

Go into an inner, relaxed state of silence and contemplation. Within the inner silence, take each negatively judgmental feeling and thought of not being good enough, and ask yourself—*How would God, Christ Jesus, Buddha, or Krishna judge my life experience and myself?* Now realize that all negative judgment, of not being good enough, is now released to, and healed within, the truth of God's higher wisdom, which has just been revealed to you.

For example—You falsely feel and think that you are not good enough, that you have failed at life because you have given your all to a love relationship and yet that relationship ceased to be all that you desired it to be. Now look at yourself and your past or present, seeming to be less than perfect, love relationship through the enlightened, understanding, non-judgmental eyes of God, Christ Jesus, Buddha, or Krishna. Perhaps you will intuitively perceive that an enlightened one would see that you did do the best you could at the time, with the level of spiritual knowledge that you had available to you at that time and under the specific circumstances in which you were involved. Perhaps you see in a clearer manner that the one you were with, for whatever reason, just was not someone who had the ability to love you in the way that you needed, deserved, desired, and so on.

Also, see if you are feeling and thinking thoughts of negative judgment about another or others, as not being good enough, and *list below*. Realize that another source of emotional, mental, spiritual, and physical stress is found in our wrong judgment of another to please us, or to do things the way that we would like them to be done. Thus, we put pressure on ourselves by having a great deal of vested energy tied into whether another person will change for the better in the exact way that we desire them to change, so that we will feel pleased, in control of another, honored, or listened to, and thus be at peace.

- _

- _

- _

- _

Go into an inner, relaxed state of silence and contemplation. Within the inner silence, take each negatively judgmental feeling and thought about another, not being good enough and ask yourself—*How would God, Christ Jesus, Buddha, or Krishna judge this individual?* Now realize that all negative judgment that you held within yourself of another is now released to, and healed within, the truth of God's higher wisdom, which has just been revealed to you.

For example—You feel a great deal of inner discontent because you perceive that another does not respect and honor you the way that you would desire to be honored and respected so that you will feel good enough about yourself! Intuitively, spiritually perceive that the enlightened wisdom of God, Christ, Buddha, or Krishna would see this individual through the elevated sight of spiritual discernment. Perhaps an enlightened one would see that this individual is incapable of really respecting you because they feel extremely unsure of who they are. So if one has little respect for oneself, then it is basically impossible for that one to have respect for someone else. Or perhaps an enlightened one would perceive that you need to respect yourself for who you are spiritually, and you no longer need respect from anyone else!

Do you feel any deep-seated sense of dissatisfaction with yourself—your life—or with others? Dissatisfaction comes from the false belief that says that something, which is necessary for my happiness and fulfillment within myself, another, or life, is missing. Now take these areas of dissatisfaction and *list below.*

- _

- _

- _

- _

Within an inner state of healing silence, realize that in your oneness with the Presence of God within your mind, heart, and life, you already have all that you need for your personal realization of inner and outer happiness and fulfillment. Then let go of all of the false feelings of dissatisfaction and be healed and be at peace.

For example—Most feelings and thoughts of dissatisfaction about yourself, another, or about your life usually have their foundation upon a deep inner sense of a lack of fulfillment. In truth, it is the Presence of God within your mind and heart that must be, and only will be, your true and lasting source of inner and outer fulfillment and satisfaction.

The more that you bring tension to your mind, through your negative thoughts and emotions, the more tension you bring to your body, which may result in illness and distressful emotions. It is time for you to completely, on all levels of your emotions and in your thought process, *take time-out!* Refuse to feel or think any thoughts or emotions of criticism, judgment, or dissatisfaction. Do this all day—do this for a week—do this for a month—until you are living an everyday lifestyle that is completely free from all harmful emotions and thoughts. *Take a vacation from negativity* to allow your body and emotions to rest and to feel good.

SECOND STEP
CONNECT WITH GOD (INNER HEALER)

Affirmation—Spiritual Principle of Truth

* Each and every time that I go into a quiet state of *Meditation*—I contact the wisdom of my inner healer, The Presence of God, The Intuitive Guidance of God, Who tells me what I need, from day to day, for renewed health and well-being.

Within each of you is the Presence of God, Who knows exactly what you need for renewed and continual good health. The Presence of God, your inner healer, knows what will make you well. The Presence of God within your mind knows what changes need to be made in your life so that you are brought back to perfect balance.

Take Time to Listen More

Listen to your internal guidance as to what your body, your emotions, your spirit, and soul needs, at this time, to feel good and to be able to realize wholeness and health. Listen to the still small voice of God, which is the internal voice of Universal wisdom, and All-knowingness. Listen to your intuition; listen to the truth of your heart so that you will be led to what you need to bring about an improved and better state of health. Each one of us has the internal knowledge of what we need in our lives so that we are healthy, happy, and whole. For to be healthy, happy, and whole is our divine birthright. So really start to sincerely listen within yourself to what intuitive ideas come to your awareness at this time of spiritualized study.

For Example

Maybe you need more time for yourself. This may be a time in your life where you need to put yourself and your spiritual growth first. This may be the perfect time to arrange for yourself a simple and enjoyable discipline of daily spiritual study and practices. This could be an exciting time to setup your daily schedule to be more spiritually oriented and simpler. For example—you may find that you enjoy getting up early before others do, sitting outside and enjoying the early morning quietness and watching the beauty and peace of the sun rising. You may feel intuitively guided to meditate several times during the day just to feel relaxed and at peace within yourself. Maybe your diet needs to be changed to one that is simpler and more satisfying to the relaxation of your entire physiological system. Conceivably you may need to be living a lifestyle that is without as much stress. It may be that this is the perfect time to simplify your life and choose the ways in which you desire to live. It could be that your life just needs to have more real meaning. Maybe this is a time for you to do that special something that you have always desired to do, to learn, or complete. Perhaps you need to ask yourself if you are really living the dreams that you hold dear to your heart so that your everyday life has more meaning and fulfillment. This may be the important time for you to change the quality of your friendships so that they are more positive, encouraging, understanding, and supportive. It is highly possible that this is the perfect time to decide to be friends with those that are really on the same spiritual path that you are, where you can really uphold each other in your own individual spiritual growth.

Remember, that what you specifically need at this time may be completely different than what another needs—so listen, listen, listen to your own inner healer. There are many books available to you that have many fine suggestions on how to attain health and wholeness, and the suggestions of others can also be highly beneficial—but remember that it is *You* that knows you the best!

Many times the illness of your body is your soul trying to get your attention so that the necessary changes within yourself and also in your outer life experience will be made. If this is so, you want to be sure that you are listening to your own internal physician at all times.

THIRD STEP
MEDITATIVE REST

When you are feeling under the weather—your body is crying out for mental, physical, and spiritual rest.

Affirmation—Spiritual Principle of Truth

• Every time that I take the time to rest within the Healing Presence of God—I am filled with the energy of healing peace which, in turn, brings healing to my Mind, Body, and Soul.

When you are feeling out of sorts—whether physically or emotionally—*meditate more often.*

Meditation Exercise

The purpose of this meditation is to rest within the internal presence of peace and to allow this inner peace to heal your body, mind, emotions, and soul.

• When you begin your morning meditation, take five minutes to let go of *every* worry, concern, and upset completely and fully. Just let God take care of everything. Realize that you of yourself know nothing, and that it is God's good pleasure to take care of everything for you, in the right way, and in divine timing. So just let all of your concerns go to the healing power of God at this time.

• Within this inner state of absolute letting-go, take five minutes to know and feel that God loves you unconditionally. Know that God has always loved you and has always cared for you.

• For an additional five minutes, know that through God's unconditional love for you—you are always under the divine care of God Who desires only health and wholeness for you at all times.

• Now rest within an inner state of peace and allow this peace into your entire being. Feel this divine peace fill your thoughts—feel this divine peace fill your emotions—and feel this divine peace fill your entire body temple. Rest in this divine healing peace for as long as you desire and then return to your world rested and rejuvenated with peace.

Continue to—Meditate more often during the day. Feel the inner peace of God. Rest in this inner peace. Bring the healing vibration of peace into all areas of your being.

• When you wake up at night—meditate on this inner healing vibration of peace.

- During the day, periodically, just close your eyes for a minute and feel this inner peace and wholeness. *Relax more!*

FOURTH STEP
LET GO AND TAKE A MENTAL VACATION

When you are really sick you tend to let go of the pressing responsibilities that are before you. Before you find yourself in this state of disharmony physically—Take a mental vacation from all pressing responsibilities.

Affirmation—Spiritual Principle of Truth

- Today and every day I mentally let go of every sense of personal responsibility and I *surrender all* to the perfect Fulfillment of God."

Daily Exercise

Today and every day—let go of every worry and know that the answers to all that concerns and worries you is now within God's All-Knowing Mind, Who is ready, willing, and delighted to reveal to you the necessary steps that are needed for the perfect healing of all of your worries and concerns. Go into a light state of meditation and intuit every worry that you feel you need to let go of at this time—for better health and well-being—and list these energy draining thoughts of worry.

- _

- _

- _

- _

Realize that each of these energy draining worries have come to your attention at this time so that they can be fully released into the healing power of the All-Knowing Mind of God. These worries are now to be released into the Mind of God, into the creative Consciousness of God, so that exceptional answers will be forthcoming. Within the Consciousness of God, in which all that has life and reality exists, there are no problems. When you let go of worry and concern and desire to have answers from the higher wisdom of God, you have opened your mind and your intuitive nature to an expansiveness of creative thought that knows only unlimited possibilities for good and absolute fulfillment. You are literally brainstorming with the Mind, the Consciousness, that created this infinite universe and all that this infinite universe contains.

Release each worry on the above list to the healing power of God's universal, All-Knowing wisdom and power. Decide that you no longer want to waste your time worrying about problems that are already being healed or already have been healed within the All-Knowing Mind, the infinite Consciousness of God. Remember that: *God is All-Power Everywhere Present and that God is All-Wisdom.* It is the All-Wisdom and All-Power of God that is perfecting every circumstance in your life now. Let go and let God fulfill your everyday responsibilities through your open, relaxed, restful, and intuitive mind, which is one with the All-Knowing Mind of God, the "All-Possibility Consciousness" of God. Now your mind is open to, and aware of, universal answers to so-called problems in an even greater degree than before. Each time that you remember to intentionally let go of your worries and to depend upon the greater universal wisdom and guidance of God to help you out, you will be further along in living your life the way that God planned you to live it. God created you and your life so that the Presence, the Consciousness, the wisdom of God can express through you so that your life can, indeed, be happier and more fulfilled.

FIFTH STEP
REEVALUATE YOUR LIFE

Affirmation—Spiritual Principle of Truth

• I take this time to look within myself and *reevaluate* my life. I choose to live every day of my life in a state of inner and outer happiness and personal satisfaction."

Daily Exercise

When we quietly and intuitively join with the intuitive wisdom of the Presence of God within ourselves and ask the greater wisdom of God for guidance, we are then open and aware to a better way of living then we were previously aware. In a quiet state of inner introspection—ask yourself these questions:

• How do I really want to live each day?

For example—You may intuitively be led to living each day in a state of inner peace and calm, knowing that the realized Presence of God within your heart is the source of all that you have need of, thus each day is truly heavenly to you. Therefore, you are living a balanced inner life each day, mentally, emotionally and spiritually, which brings balance to your physical body.

• What do I really want to do?

For Example—You may intuitively be guided to make a change in your occupation. Perhaps you now see that the work that you are doing at this time is not fully satisfying to you. So now you open your mind to further daily guidance from the universal guidance of God to lead you in the daily steps that are necessary for you to make the changes that you need to make, in the proper way, and at the proper time.

• What will bring health into my life?

For Example—You may be intuitively guided to read a certain book on diet. This may be a new diet, which is in greater harmony with the vibrational field of your specific body temple than any previous book, or diet that you have heard about.

• How can I feel really fulfilled right now?

For Example—You may be intuitively guided to realize that *now* is the perfect time for you to emotionally stop all outer searching for fulfillment. Now is the time for you to discover that—within your *personally-realized oneness with the Presence of God*, which resides within your mind and heart—there resides the ultimate spiritual truth that will set you free. This truth that will set you free is found within an inner absolute knowingness, which perceives that—*In your oneness with the Presence of God, you are already fulfilled*.

• What goals do I have before me that fill me with a sense of excitement?

For Example—You may now intuitively know that a worthy goal for you to undertake at this time is to immerse yourself into an area of spiritual study, perhaps holistic healing, and study the many and varied sources of information available on this enlivening and useful subject until they become an exciting and natural part of your everyday lifestyle. When you have honestly answered these important questions—see where you can make the necessary changes in your life, which are totally appropriate for you.

SIXTH STEP
FEEL THE HEALING ENERGY OF WHOLENESS

To feel good, you need to start to feel good within—first

Affirmation—Spiritual Principle of Truth

• I am One with the Perfection and Wholeness of God—which is the state of *inner health* that I now feel completely throughout my entire being.

Daily Exercise

Make a list of what makes you feel good. Think about the times that you felt really great—what were you doing, how were you living your life, what friend-ships did you have, in what activities were you involved?

• _

• _

• _

Now see what is missing in your life, from the above list, which is causing you to be out of balance and write these down.

• _

• _

• _

Compare both lists and see where you can make the necessary changes, then write down the necessary steps that you are now guided to take.

• _

- _

- _

For Example—You simply see that in the past, your work schedule allowed you to exercise every day at the neighborhood gym, which filled you with a great sense of inner and outer fulfillment. You now see that your new work schedule has restricted your ability (time-wise) to go to the gym, thus you realize that daily exercise is lacking in your new set of circumstances. So you intuitively perceive that you would be better off taking the time to walk every day, and you intellectually discern that you can do this if you get up early every morning and go for a refreshing and invigorating walk.

Do this same exercise for your emotional health. Whenever you feel depressed or just out of it—make a list of the times when you felt really wonderful and alive, emotionally.

What was your life like and what were you doing?

- _

- _

- _

See what is missing now, and bring back to yourself the missing steps and ingredients that are necessary for your emotional well-being and health.

- _

- _

- _

For Example—You now discern that the times when you were emotionally happy and fulfilled were times when you intentionally took the time in the morning to really look forward to the day that was before you. Now you find that you have gotten into the bad habit of emotionally resenting the day that is before you because of all of the work that you have to do. Now you intuitively perceive that you need to take your emotional life in hand and intentionally dedicate the day before you, and every activity that is before you, to the glory of the Presence of

God working through you—thus bringing a real sense of divine excellence to your day.

SEVENTH STEP
UNITE WITH THE HEALING POWER OF JOY

To be healthy, emotionally and physically, you need to have a good and healthy sense of joy in your life.

Affirmation—Spiritual Principle of Truth

• I take several moments of quiet time—to be intuitively led to the activities that will fill me with the *healing vibrations of wholeness*.

When you are doing what you enjoy—this releases the healing vibrations of joy and relaxation which fill you with the realization of completion, which brings you back to a perfect state of well-being and inner and outer health.

Many times in life we can easily get caught up in the everyday responsibilities to work and to others, which may cause us to forget that we also have a life that needs to be joyful and fun. Thus, it is important to take time periodically and ask yourself what activities would bring to you a sincere feeling of joy at this time.

Joy is One of the Greatest Healing Tools that You Can Use

Take a few moments to yourself and let yourself see, with your inner sight, what it is that you really desire to do at this time in your life. Ask yourself—*If you could do any enjoyable activity, this day, or this week, or this month, what would you be doing? If you only had you to answer to, how would you spend your time?*

Daily Exercise—

Each day do something that you *really enjoy*—read a good book, walk in nature, have lunch with a good friend, watch an uplifting movie, etc. Look at your list of special enjoyments that have real meaning to you, and see where you can start to put them into daily practice.

> *Feeling out of balance or feeling under the weather is the way that your soul and body is telling you to be good to yourself—for you are the only self that you have.*

HEALING MEDITATION

- As I come into the Presence of God that is within my heart and mind—I come with the inner feeling of peace and oneness. In this special oneness, I am filled with the healing vibrations of wholeness and well-being.

- In the Presence of God—I hear the voice of God speaking—words of wisdom to me—which guide me in making the right decisions and changes in my life that are necessary for me to have good health in all areas of my life.

- In my oneness with the divine presence of health and wholeness, I am now healed of all that is in the way of my finding fulfillment in this lifetime.

- Thank you Divine Presence, within my heart and soul, for the beautiful life that I now have before me. I am whole, perfect, and secure in the truth of perfect health and well-being within my mind, body, and soul

And So It Is!

8

The Mystical Marriage

How to Have A True Mystical Marriage with God
How to Have A True Mystical Marriage with Another
How to Recognize a Soul-Mate
How to Maintain and Elevate A True Mystical Marriage

Author's note: The following lesson has been personally worked with and divinely interpreted from the truth of the teachings of Christ, which reveal the following realities of our Divine Selfhood.

To live in a state of a mystical marriage, you must first of all love the Presence of God within yourself with your whole mind, heart, and being, and be able to love another as you love yourself, or in better words, to love another as you wish another to love you.

During the Last Supper Christ said that he was giving to us a new commandment, and that momentous pronouncement was to love each other as God loves us. When we allow the unconditional love of God to love through us, then we are truly loving others as God loves us.

Love is one of the most important aspects of our lives. Being with the one that is our perfect mate brings real meaning into our lives. Following are clues for spiritually recognizing your special soul-mate, together with elevating and maintaining a current or future soul-mate relationship through true, spiritualized, divine love.

Whether you already have a soul-mate relationship or if you are looking for a soul-mate relationship—we can all agree that most of us, from our teenage years onward, have always been yearning deep down inside of ourselves for union with our perfect mate, for union with that perfect *someone* who is just right for us. And as a result of finding this perfect someone, we sincerely hope that we will live in a heavenly state of marital bliss throughout our lives together!

The need or longing for love—the need and longing to be freely loved and to be able to love freely in return—is our inherent desire to be centered within the realm of unconditional love which resides in our own hearts.

Within a love relationship we long to find the attainment of unconditional love—which we are really seeking from God—with another. When we finally realize that such yearning and longing to find completion with another is actually our soul yearning to reunite with God, then we are free to find and unite with God's unconditional love within ourselves. Then, and only then, can we seek to outwardly express and share, this divine love with the heart of another—who has also found their own inner completeness within themselves through their conscious realization of *oneness with God* within their own heart.

It is through the vehicle of a committed love relationship, a potentially mystical marriage, that we put to the test and refine the quality of unconditional love within ourselves. Through our human love relationships, we come face-to-face with the areas within ourselves that need to be worked on further—that need to be spiritually fined-tuned—so that we come to know that we are filled with an inner state of unconditional love that can never be depleted.

- The spiritual definition of a mystical marriage is to mate and to have union with the Presence of God within ourselves. The ability to have a real mystical marriage with another human being is found within our desire to seek union with the Presence of God within our own hearts, and there rest within the contentment of God's unconditional love, which nothing can be taken from nor added to our state of inner fulfillment and contentment.

- From this inner state of *Divine Ecstasy* (inner contentment and inner peace) we find ourselves desiring to express and share this unconditionally divine love of God, which we find within our own hearts, with another of like heart.

- The spiritual purpose of having a mystical marriage is to be able to have inner union with the Presence of God within ourselves, and union with the Presence of God within another for the purpose of attaining added spiritual growth and fulfillment.

BASIC TYPES OF SOUL-MATES

There are many esoteric views and definitions about the meaning of soul-mates—but this specific teaching will cover what I have found to be the practical aspect of having a soul-mate relationship. Included will be the mystical views of a soul-mate relationship, that I have taken into deep meditation and there realized the everyday workability of these truths, which can be used successfully in our everyday life experiences. I have found that these truths have worked in my own life and in the lives of many others.

• A soul-mate relationship is a relationship where you are drawn to another for added experience and soul growth. The one that you are attracted to depends on the choice of life lessons that each of you has decided to complete in this life.

• A soul-mate relationship may be one in which you come together with another of like mind and soul because you both have a *Pre-Destined Purpose* together—a common goal of service to humanity.

• In the majority of cases, a true soul-mate relationship is where you find that you are in harmony with another because of the *sameness* of interests and personality traits. *In this case, you may have several potential soul-mates with whom you are in harmony. If this happens, you will need to choose which one is the most harmonious with you at the present time and simultaneously intuitively-perceive which one will continue to be in harmony with you in the future.* This last definition of a soul-mate is the most prevalent of all for most people who are on the spiritual path.

The sameness of personality traits and interests in life helps to bring a balance of compatible energies to a potential soul-mate relationship for the following reasons:

• We all emit energies, vibrations, or certain frequencies. Just like a radio, we all transmit and receive.

• We all emit energies on the surface level of who we are—our body, our clothes, the way we move, the way we look, and so on.

• We also emit energies from a deeper level of who we are—our thoughts, our beliefs, and our experiences.

- We also emit energies that originate from our true Spiritual-Soul-Nature. We are emitting the energies present in our level of consciousness, which are gained through our daily meditation and spiritual study.

- We emit the energies and vibrations of our life's purpose here on earth.

- We all emit energies of our true spiritual God-Self and our human false-self out to the world around us.

Principle—

Your soul-mate is one who is on your own basic *energy level* because of the compatibility of your inner natures. One who is on your energy level is one that you will feel good around—one where you will feel that you are completely and freely being your real self when you are with them—one with whom you will feel completely accepted!

Daily Exercise—Ideal or Concept to Work With—

Become aware of how you feel around different people. Do you feel comfortable or uncomfortable? Do you feel as if you can really be yourself, or do you have the need to put on an act or be different from whom you really are? Do you feel absolutely accepted and acknowledged, or do you feel criticized and belittled? *Be Aware!*

PART ONE
GUIDE TO RECOGNIZING YOUR SOUL-MATE

Quality Found in A True Soul-Mate Relationship

Harmony—There must be an 80% to a 100% agreement—alignment between the two of you concerning your basic beliefs about life and the goals that you want to attain together in your relationship. You both have agreement between your views of religion, politics, raising of children, and your beliefs about life and human nature in general.

- Both of you are who you are, with no role-playing. Refuse to be any less than who you really are!

- There is no criticizing of each other. There is a lack of arrogance in your attitude towards each other. There is a lack of impatience in dealing with each other.

- You are both in tune with each other. You both have similar beliefs about morals; your thoughts are similar; your belief system is similar. You are both in agreement about the style of living that you will have together. You are both in agreement about your work life and the life roles that each of you will play out.

Exercise of Acceptance—

Whenever you come into the presence of someone of whom you feel critical, take a deep breath and accept them just the way they are. Remember that we usually feel critical, annoyed, or uncomfortable around another person because we are both feeling and expressing, from our personal, emotional, and soul selves; conflicting, varying, and different energies or frequencies of self-expression. Harmonize and heal the varying energies between the two of you by harmonizing your energies through the intentional exercise of *just accepting* the other person as they are.

You are Both Best Friends—Your soul-mate relationship starts out on the level of friendship and this friendship continues throughout your life together. Your soul-mate is your best friend!

- Your soul communicates first with the other's soul, and then physical harmony is brought into this communion. We build a true soul-mate relationship on the level of friendship and companionship, which leads to physical attraction and appreciation.

Equality Exercise—There is an inner sureness and knowingness of equality between soul-mates. They are equals on all levels of spirituality, intelligence, and expression. In your soul-mate relationship, you must establish equality and honor for one another.

- Men—honor the woman in your life—honor *who she uniquely* is and what she offers.

Equality Exercise—Take a quiet time of contemplative meditation and feel the Presence of God. Feel your oneness with the quality of divine equality, and see in your mind's eye a woman that you know. Feel your oneness, your divine equality with this woman during your meditative practice. When you see this woman in person—bring to your conscious remembrance the feeling of divine equality that you experienced in meditation. And, express the outer realization of this quality of divine equality to her as you interact.

- Women—honor the man in your life—honor *who he uniquely* is and what he has to offer.

Equality Exercise—Take a quiet time of contemplative meditation and feel the Presence of God. Feel your oneness with the quality of divine equality, and see in your mind's eye a man that you know. Feel your oneness, your divine equality with this man during your meditative practice. When you see this man in person—bring to your conscious remembrance the feeling of divine equality that you experienced in meditation. And, express the outer realization of this quality of divine equality to him as you interact.

- Honor Thy Soul-Mate Always! Stop any words or feelings of resentment, and criticizing of differences, before they start! *Honor the Difference!*

Unified—Soul-mates complement each other's qualities and talents. Soul-Mates always uplift each other!

- Soul-mates are so in harmony with each other that they actually have the same, or similar, talents and gifts. Soul-mates are a real working team with each other on many levels.

Freedom of Self-Expression—When soul-mates have joined together—they both express their true and whole selves completely.

- There is no need for any protection of self-expression in a true soul-mate relationship. Each person is balanced and whole because of their joining together with their soul-mate.

Soul Communication—Soul-mates speak the same language. Soul-mates speak to each other from their hearts, minds, and souls.

- Soul-mates always speak the truth to each other. There is no need or compulsion for any sort of manipulation, control, or game playing of any kind. Soul-mates are always in tune with each other on an intellectual, spiritual, and emotional level.

- Soul-mates even know what the other is thinking and feeling—they have the same, or similar, emotions—the same, or similar, reactions to life—the same, or similar, likes and dislikes about weather, food, entertainment, and so on.

- Soul-mates always speak kindly to one another! If they were ever unkind or critical to each other, they would know that they were really being unkind and critical of a part of themselves. *Soul-Mates are an extension of each other.*

PART TWO
HOW TO MAINTAIN AND ELEVATE A TRUE SOUL-MATE RELATIONSHIP BE IN A CONTINUAL STATE OF UNCONDITIONAL LOVE

Meditation—

Each day be sure to join with the unconditional love energy of God within the center of your heart. Take at least five minutes in the morning and just allow yourself to feel, to be one with God's divine, unconditional love.

Periodically during the day, regardless of how you feel or what is going on that appears to be of a negative nature, take time to yourself to close your eyes and really feel, really allow yourself to be filled with, and connect with the Unconditional Love of God within your heart center.

> *Unconditional love is a love that has no conditions attached to it. Unconditional love is a divine love that freely expresses itself without expecting anything in return. Unconditional love is a love that is always within your heart center, freely flowing out to the one that you love regardless of whether they are expressing love to you at the present moment or not.*

- **Send Unconditional Love to Yourself**—Each day take time to send the kind of unconditional love to yourself that you would like to receive in return. Within the realm of spiritual truth—you are the only one that is responsible for loving yourself unconditionally. It is imperative that you take time to yourself and allow the Presence of God within your heart to love yourself as God's special and unique expression of divine life.

SPIRITUALIZED COMMUNICATION

Morning Love Meditation—

- **Each morning**—as soon as you attain any kind of wakefulness join your heart to the Heart of God. Inwardly see within your mind's eye, feel, and realize that your human heart is now replaced with the universal, unconditionally loving and All-understanding Heart of God. You are now feeling the Presence of God's unconditional love within your heart and flowing through your heart. Rest in God's pure Heart, which is filled to overflowing with unconditional love. Rest in God's pure Heart, which seeks only the best for you and the best for those that you love. Seek to keep alive, within your heart center, this high quality of unconditional love during the whole day by intuitively knowing and feeling that it is now God's Heart that is loving through your human heart.

- **Before you speak**—Take a moment to feel the unconditional love that the Presence of God within your heart feels for the loved one with whom you are about to speak. Allow the unconditional love of God to influence every word that you are about to speak so that you are speaking words that originate from a pure inner sense of harmlessness. Sincerely desire to bless your loved one with every word that you speak.

- **Anger, resentment, hurt, manipulation**—Whenever you find yourself in a negative state of anger, resentment, hurt, or in a manipulative state that needs to control your loved one or needs to get your loved one to do something that they do not want to do—Say Nothing! Take a few minutes to yourself to reconnect with the unconditional love of God within your heart and seek the All-wisdom and divine understanding of God's Presence to speak through you. Only speak from a heart that is pure and free from any harmful motive or intent to hurt, control, or manipulate another.

- **Put yourself in your loved one's shoes**—Continually seek God's guidance from the center of your heart where, God's unconditional love is flowing forth as to what your loved one is feeling, and how you can best bring to them a greater sense of peace and contentment through the words that you speak to them.

- **As you give so do you receive**—Most people still find themselves being and living in a state of *unaware* humanhood. The state of unaware humanhood is an emotional state that is extremely reactionary. Thus, the majority of people that you encounter will react in the same manner to you as you initially treat them. Knowing this basic human principle, or way of reaction, will help you in your ability to lovingly encourage people who are close to you to treat and react to you in a loving and harmonious manner.

- **Look at your current relationship** and decide how you would like your loved one to treat you, and make a list. Take each trait on your list and work on developing and expressing that trait yourself. As you work on these desired traits yourself, know that others who are close to you usually react to, and express, the same emotional and spiritual traits that you are personally expressing. For example—If you find that you desire greater peace in your relationship with your loved one, you will need to work on finding that quality of peace within yourself first (not seeking peace at all from your loved one) and work on expressing this quality of peace throughout your relationship even when your loved one seems to be in a less than peaceful mood!

- **Look at your life with your loved one** and see where you feel that certain desired emotional traits are missing, write them down, and work on being and expressing these qualities yourself. Very simply, if you want more love, then give more love. If you want more appreciation, then give appreciation. If you want to be listened to, then become a better listener yourself. If you want your loved one to be happy in the morning, then work on being really happy in the morning yourself. And on and on the list can go!

If you are having a time of disharmony within an already existing love relationship, work with the following exercise.

At the conclusion of your meditation periods, and periodically during the day, feel yourself being divinely guided as to "how to" perfect and harmonize your soul-mate relationship. Be open and receptive to any healing ideas that the All-knowing Mind of God intuitively sends to you. Know and trust that you are always being guided by the All-wisdom of God in your search for, and demonstration of, a perfect and harmonious love relationship. Continue to know that the will of God for you is that you be truly loved for who you are. Always trust that the All-knowing Mind of God really does know what is best for you and your loved one.

PART THREE
GUIDE TO ATTRACTING YOUR SOUL-MATE
MEDITATE DAILY

I know that God is the Presence and source of unconditional love in my life.

Meditation Exercise—Meditate on your oneness with God each day to realize the truth of who you are.

- Each morning before you get up and every evening before you drift off to sleep, go into a deep and relaxing state of mind and body and feel your oneness with the unconditional love of God.

- In this state of unconditional love, sincerely desire to really know *God, as the Presence of unconditional love in your life.* Let the Presence of all that God's unconditional love is, fill you completely. Then rest in the realization of who you really are, knowing that you are made in the image and likeness of God's unconditional love.

Visualization Exercise—At the closing of your Meditation see the reality of who you truly are as the unique expression of the unconditional love of God, and visualize an energy or vibrational field of unconditional love going out from you and connecting with that special someone, and everyone, that is in the highest harmony with you.

- You need to know your true God-Self—your balanced Self—your spiritual Self—which will then attract to you your real soul-mate. Only by really knowing who you are, will you be able to express to others the truth of who you are. Only by spending time within yourself, through the tool of daily meditation, will you take the time that is necessary to know yourself inside and out.

RADIATE YOUR LOVE ENERGY DAILY

As I freely feel and live in my own love atmosphere, as I freely give out this love atmosphere to all, in turn, do I receive this high quality of divine love from others.?

Dedicate yourself to feeling the divine love of God that you have personally experienced during your morning meditation, throughout the entire day, and continue to do so throughout the entire evening. The divine unconditional love that you have within your heart is the truth of who you are, and the ability to live in the continual atmosphere of unconditional love is the truth of the quality of life that you are to be living. It is your right, as the divine creation of God, to be living in a continual state of unconditional love, and to be living in the continual atmosphere of heaven on earth, right here and right now. It is your choice and your divine right to do so.

The divine love atmosphere that you choose to live in is an atmosphere that is highly attractive to others who are around you. When you are living in the atmosphere of unconditional love, other people of like spiritual nature are naturally drawn to that quality of love that resonates with their own heart nature. Then you will find yourself receiving from others, of like mind and heart, the same spiritual quality of unconditional love that you are radiating out to others.

Throughout the day, silently and enthusiastically say to yourself—

- I freely radiate the unconditional love within my heart to the world around me! *And watch for the world of unconditional love to awaken, to come to life all around you!*

GIVE THE GIFT OF YOUR LOVE

In my daily activities I now vibrate Love, which attracts back to me—others of like love—like consciousness—and like mind."

The conscious effort that we give to the energy that we vibrate to, goes out into the universe to bring back to us the perfection on which we focus. When you are thinking and feeling negative thoughts and experiencing feelings of fear, lack, hopelessness, anger, etc., you vibrate to a negative energy that is repelling to others. When you are thinking and feeling positive thoughts, and experiencing feelings of love, joy, peace, contentment, etc., you vibrate to a positive energy that draws others to you that are of: like love, like consciousness, and like mind.

During the day, be sure to express and feel positive emotions and thoughts that attract positive energy to you—versus being an individual who is expressing and feeling negativity.

Positiveness exercise—Before your start your day, and periodically during the day, close your eyes and feel an inner feeling of love, peace, joy, and contentment, until you literally feel yourself vibrating with these positive energies!

SURRENDER YOUR WILL TO THE WILL OF GOD

I surrender my will to the All-Loving, All-Knowing Will of God, and I trust God (the Universe) to bring Fulfillment to my love life.

Let Go and Trust! Many times you may actually keep yourself from knowing the perfect relationship just because of your inner feelings of hopelessness, fear, and doubt. Know that the Presence of God within you will attract the Presence of God within the one that is perfect for you! Refuse to entertain any feelings of fear or loneliness. God's will for you is filled with love.

Healing of Fear Exercise—Every time that you feel yourself worrying about your relationship, worrying whether you will ever have a real love relationship, or worrying that a current relationship will ever have the quality of love that you desire—take time to consciously turn within to the Presence of God and know that God's will for you is one of love. Get the energy of your personal fear and worry out of the picture. Realize, calmly, during the times that you find yourself in the negative energy of fear and loneliness—that this state of fear and loneliness is not necessary for you to go through anymore! Refuse to be a victim of fear and loneliness from this day forward, and declare that you are one with the love-filled vision that God has for you.

- To the degree that you are able to turn away from the feeling of fear to an inner state of calm and positive certainty—you will heal any negative emotions that may be keeping love from you. And, at the very least, you will feel much better and content about yourself and the life that you are living.

HAVE A POSITIVE FOCUS

Each day I choose to be the energy of unconditional love in all that I am and in all that I do.

Each day that you live should be lived to the fullest, regardless of the state of your love life. Each soul has certain circumstances to go through in this lifetime, and each of us is given the wonderful gift of this life to live as successfully as possible. The main aspect of success in this life is to be able to love and to be loved in return, even if that means simply loving the Presence of God within yourself, loving who you really are, or just unconditionally loving and appreciating the little boy that delivers your morning newspaper. *Just the simple act of intentionally feeling appreciation and love for the neighborhood paper boy, day after day, will fill you with a love for life that will transform your capacity for expressing love within yourself, on a continuous level.* A spiritually successful life means that you have the capacity to love unconditionally. To love unconditionally means that you love others even when others do not love you. Loving unconditionally means that you find ways to just love others in your life whether or not they represent a real or potential love relationship. The greatest joy we can develop in this life is to have the ability to be in a continual state of inner unconditional love regardless of what our outer life looks like.

Every day be alert to ways that you may give the outer manifestation of love to others. Be alert to the many opportunities that come to you each day, especially when you are alert and aware, to give the gifts of—

- Courtesy—saying please and thank you to those that you do business with and with members of your family and close friends.

- Kindness—helping someone to feel good about themselves when they seem down in spirits.

- Consideration—really desiring to know what someone close to you wants to do for a day of joy and fun.

- Expressing forgiving and understanding patience to others—being intentionally understanding and forgiving when another is short-tempered and unkind with you.

As you give of the love that is within you, even in small ways, this quality of divine love multiples, and, in turn, attracts more love to you in whatever circumstance of life you find yourself at the present moment. *Look for infinite opportunities to give the outer manifestation of love today!*

- To the degree that you feel the possibility of perfect love in your life, you will allow this high quality of love to enter into your experience. Remember to continue to focus on the positive always and *Never Give Up Hope!!*

TRUST GOD ABSOLUTELY

I let go of all worry, fear, and concern. I now Trust God—the creator of this Universe to bring to me my perfect Soul-mate for this life—in the right way—at the right time—and under the right circumstances.

Our perfect soul-mate may not be in our life at this time for many good reasons. Our soul-mate may be unconsciously waiting for the perfect time to unite with us as far as both of our spiritual growth processes go. Trust God, and all will be well, happy, and perfect.

Healing Of Negativity Exercise—Whenever you feel any sense of fear, worry, or concern—instantly let go of all worry, fear, and concern—and instantly let your whole heart, mind, and soul Trust God, the creator of this universe, to bring to you your perfect soul-mate for this life—in the right way—at the right time—and under the right circumstances.

HEALING MEDITATION

- Today I come into the Presence of God at the center of my heart; and here I place my absolute trust in God for the fulfillment of love in my life.

- All of the deepest and grandest desires of my heart are now being fulfilled in the right way and at the right time for I am one with the All-Wisdom of God.

- I now rest in a feeling of complete trust and relaxation—knowing that God will bring about the best results for the coming together of myself and the perfect spiritual mate for which I yearn.

- I am now in a complete feeling of peace, for I am assured that God's Presence, within me, is actively working through me to bring to me the perfect answers to all of the needs for love that I now have, or ever will have in the future.

- I give complete and absolute thanks that my love life is now being made manifest, in an absolute vibration of fulfillment and eternal happiness.

And So It Is!

9

Lighten Up, Let Go, and Let God Run Your Life

How to Lighten Up Your Serious Side

Author's note: The following lesson has been personally worked with and divinely interpreted from the truth of the teachings of Christ, which reveal the following realities of our Divine Selfhood.

I of my own self can do nothing; it is the Father—the presence of God—within me that do all of these good works.

I trust that the Presence of God within me will guide and direct all my ways. I trust that the Presence of God will show me how to live my life in wondrously profound ways, which will enrich this ongoing journey that I call life.

God, this is your day and I courageously dedicate myself to freely rejoice and be exceedingly glad in it!

I live my life—not by the dictates of this world of need—but by every word of divine truth and hope that proceeds from the mouth—the Mind and Heart—of God.

I promise to free myself from all worry about my life—for I know that God knows what I have need of and that it is God's good pleasure to lead me into the "Ever Abundant Kingdom of Fulfillment."

Perhaps you find yourself from time to time, being a very organized, perfection-driven individual who seems to be always striving for the best and the highest within yourself and within your life. Yet, from time to time, you know that it is important to lighten-up, because you are taking too much responsibility for yourself and your life. Whenever you feel this inner sense of stress, you can always turn quickly within to the Presence of God in meditation, so that you can let go and be guided by the wisdom of God within your heart and mind.

Contained within this lesson is the guidance that I received from my daily meditations on this very important subject. Within the following series of lessons, I will share with you the principles that I intuitively received from the higher wisdom and guidance of God on how to lighten-up spiritually.

The major spiritual principle that is involved with the issue of letting-go; letting God take over your life; lightening-up on yourself, is the Principle of Divine Trust. If you can trust the God that created this universe to have the sun rise every morning and to have the sun set every evening, then you can absolutely trust this divine wisdom to guide you in the successful living of your life.

Christ Jesus said—*"I of my own self can do nothing, it is the Father within me that does all of these good works."* You and I, very often take much to much responsibility for the harmonious running of our lives. Yes, we do need to do what needs to be done, and yes, we do need to be responsible and accountable for this life that we are living, but it is the *Divine Presence of God Expressing Throught Us* that brings real fulfillment and success into our lives.

When you are up-tight and unnecessarily serious you actually get in the way of the supreme Plan for Good that God has in store for you. You actually put a stop to the Presence of God working in your life to bring about the perfect events that are for your highest good. Being up-tight and unnecessarily serious brings the emotional energy of worry into your life, which, in turn, tends to suffocate the Divine Plan for Good that God has in mind for you.

Your human life experience is actually the experience of God—when you lighten-up and let God live through you to the fullest. Life at times can seem very stressful and full of worries and concerns—but that is the exact time to lighten-up and let the Presence of God bring harmony into all areas of your life.

Today is the day to decide to let your life experience be guided by the supreme, All-knowing wisdom of God. Now is the moment to make a definite decision to bring the partnership of God into all the areas of your life where there is worry, concern, and doubt. When you let the Presence of God within you take over, then you will firmly see one miracle after another take place within yourself, in your life, and in the lives of your family and loved ones.

Life becomes very exciting when you can really lighten-up and let go of all worry and doubt, for it is then that you start to see the clarity of the Vision of God which shows to you the true meaning of your life.

Your life is one that is meant to be a living tribute to the magnificence of divinity. But you will only see this truth when you are brave enough to really let God and spiritual principle work in your life completely.

SEVEN STEPS AND AFFIRMATIONS

Following are seven steps, affirmations, and exercises to use and work with, every day for a week, a month, or for however long you choose to help you lighten-up so that the full power of God can work freely in your affairs.

STEP ONE
AFFIRMATION AND EXERCISES

Lighten Up—Affirmation

• I intentionally Lighten Up and Let Go—which frees up the Power of God within my heart and mind to successfully guide me to the perfect outcome to all questions and problems in my life.

STEPS THAT WILL HELP YOU REALLY LET GO!

Make a determined effort to let go of every concern that you now have by using the following meditation exercise.

Meditative Healing Exercise—

• Become still, and feel that you are one with the Presence of God's All-love and care. View your life at this time, and intentionally let go of every concern that you now have. Know that every concern and worry that you now have has a positive answer, a positive outcome, within the All-knowing Mind of God. And inwardly know that—in proportion to your ability to really let go, right now, all of your worries and concerns to the All-knowing wisdom of God to answer and heal—you are free.

- Experience the feeling of freedom that you now have within your mind—within your emotions—and within your body. Now relax further, and let the divine inspiration of God lead you to the right answers.

Every time that you feel yourself become tense and worried—take time out to have a brief meditation—just to relax—to turn your mind into the Mind of God—so that you are receptive to divine input. Intentionally bring yourself into the inner state of freedom—where you are able to hear—intuitively—the guidance of God.

Step Two
Affirmation and Exercises

Trust—Affirmation

- I trust the wisdom and love of God to bring about complete harmony and fulfillment into my life right now. I am open to the wisdom of God to guide me at all times.

Steps Towards Developing Real Trust

Look at every area in your life that you are concerned with and make a "Personal Healing List." Know that all of the problems that you are placing on your personal healing list are going straight to the healing Mind of God, Who knows no limitation. Let go of each item on your personal healing list and let God take it over to be healed through the All-knowing, All-wisdom, and All-power of God's Presence working through you and your life.

- Give each need on your personal healing list to the Mind of God to heal. Think of God as your own personal "Healing Practitioner." Expect Healing, Expect Miracles, Trust God to make all things right!

- -

- -

Every time that you find yourself concerned over anything that is on your *Personal Healing List*—immediately turn it over to God—saying to yourself—

- I refuse to worry about this any longer! This concern is now within the All-knowing Mind of God to work out and heal in the best way possible!

STEP THREE
AFFIRMATION AND EXERCISES

Surrender—Affirmation

- I surrender my life—I surrender my limited will and intellect—I surrender my ego and pride—to the All-Knowing, All-Seeing, All-Powerful Mind of God—which allows my life to be made perfect and whole.

STEPS FOR DIVINE SURRENDER

Most of the time our sense of worry comes from feeling that we are responsible for making the right decisions that will bring about the healing of any and all problem areas in our life. So this is the time to surrender, completely, any sense of the personal ego that says it is totally your responsibility to come up with the right answer to this or any problem in your life. Remember—It is God that sees the over-all picture of what is right for you personally. So *let go and surrender* your whole life to the higher wisdom of God.

- Every morning before you get out of bed—take a quiet moment of meditation—and surrender your whole day to the perfect control of God's Divine Wisdom. Put your day into the hands of God. Let God's wisdom live through you all day long—every moment.

- In the evening before you go to sleep—thank the wisdom of the universe (God) for the perfect day that you just had. Constantly remind yourself that your life is the life of God in expression!

STEP FOUR
AFFIRMATION AND EXERCISES

Faith—Affirmation

- "I have the faith of a grain of mustard seed. I have the faith that will see through all that this life brings to me to be divinely healed. My faith gives to me the ability to see above all limitation."

STEPS FOR THE HEALING OF LIMITATION

Take a strong stand—and know—that every area of limitation that comes to your conscious mind—is a lie! Be strong!

Healing of The False Power of Limitation Exercise—

- Become still and close your eyes. Think of and list any area in your life where you feel that you are limited in any manner. For example, do you feel that you are without the intelligence that is needed to express your highest God-Self in life?

- -

- -

Every issue that comes to you of limitation is coming to you to be healed. You heal that illusion of limitation by declaring the truth about it. Rise above every problem by knowing that the spiritual truth is the only power operating in your life, and *be strong*. Heal the problem by realizing that the spiritual truth of God is All-power—All-wisdom—All-presence, and then let the problem go and move on in the sureness of harmony and fulfillment.

Take each item on your list of limitations and write down the spiritual healing truth of that so-called limitation. For example, you felt lacking or limited by the need for a higher level of personal intellect. Now state in a positive manner that it is the unlimited intelligence of God that flows through your mind, at all times!

- -

- -

Daily—go over the healing truth of each false limitation on you're above list and meditate upon the spiritual truth of each limitation until you are healed of its limiting presence once and for all! Periodically, list your perceptions of personal limitation and work on healing them in the precise manner just mentioned. Continue to keep your consciousness free of all false issues of limitation throughout your entire life.

STEP FIVE
AFFIRMATION AND EXERCISES

God's Love—Affirmation

- In my daily meditation—I rest in the absolute love of God—wherein I realize that the love of God is the answer to any problem that may be before me.

STEPS FOR UNCONDITIONAL LOVE
REALIZED—MEDITATION

- **In Meditation**—Rest for 20 minutes and remember—think about—ponder—and meditate on this truth—

GOD REALLY LOVES ME!

- Really realize that God cares about every area of your life and nothing is too small or too insignificant for the Presence of God to make right.

- Realize that you are the creation of God. Your life is the life of God. Your daily experience is the daily experience of the Presence of God living through you. God cares! Then slowly return to your daily life.

Use this powerfully healing meditation every time that you feel less than fully loved. Much of your unrest and stress is the result of feeling that you are not good enough—the feeling and/or belief, that you need to be better to be worthy of love. This false concept can only be healed by joining with the healing Presence of God's unconditional love—whenever—you feel less than perfectly loved and lovable.

STEP SIX
AFFIRMATION AND EXERCISES

Divine Purpose—Affirmation

- I am now fearless—because I know that my DIVINE PURPOSE is to live the best life that is possible. When I turn within to the Presence of God—I am filled with the fearlessness of God.

STEPS FOR THE ACHIEVEMENT OF PERFECTION

- Your purpose in life is to be the divine expression of all that God is. It is through your divine uniqueness that God is seen and experienced by others.

- Your purpose is to be the living expression of the perfection of the Creator of this universe.

- Your purpose is to be living the perfect life, so that your life is a supreme example to others of the presence, power, and great love of God.

Your duty is to live a perfect life so that you can be a light to the world around you—so lighten-up! Each day, act as if your divine purpose in life is to be an example of one who is One with God. Thus, you are the living example of one who is serene in their expression of their divine perfection.

STEP SEVEN
AFFIRMATION AND EXERCISES

Determination—Affirmation

- I am determined to live my life from this day forward by the divine Presence of God's Wisdom leading my life. I let no one enter into my consciousness to take from me my peace, sureness, and serenity.

STEPS FOR MAKING THE SPIRITUAL TRUTH A REALITY

You have all heard the expression—"Practice makes perfect." In your spiritual life, this saying is even more to the point. When you are working on a spiritual principle, that principle becomes a living truth within yourself, and in your life, when you are challenged. Every time that you are challenged with an imperfect picture of yourself—instantly realize the spiritual truth about your perfection, and stick with it!!!

When you start to live your life by really letting-go, lightening-up, and trusting the wisdom of God to run your life harmoniously, you will find yourself becoming aware of all those others who still want to worry and be fearful. This is when you need to be strong in the spiritual truth that you know.

Be sure that your life is being perfectly guided by the Divine Wisdom of God. Let no one enter into your mind—who brings you back to the false acceptance of fear, worry, and belief in limitation and disaster. For in saving yourself—by letting God run your life—you save the world.

HEALING MEDITATION

- As I become still within my mind, within my emotions, and within my very Soul, I wholeheartedly and honestly let go of all of the concerns and worries that I have at this time in my life.

- I realize that I of myself do not know what is the right answer to the problem or problems that I may have at this time. But I do know that the Presence of

God within my mind and heart does know all things. I do know that the Presence of God within my mind and heart does know the right direction that my life is to be taking.

- I affirm, that the Presence of God within my mind and heart has a perfect divine plan for my life that is now being intuitively presented to my conscious awareness. And I rest in this inner trust that I now have.

- I affirm, that I trust, completely, the Presence of God that is within me and all around me to bring and keep my life in perfect balance and fulfillment. For I continue to declare that the Presence of God's All-perfection, All-wisdom, and All-presence is the *only power* in my life this day and every day!

- I affirm, that I trust completely the Presence of God, which is within each one of us, and is around all of us, to bring and keep the lives of my loved ones in perfect balance and fulfillment. And I continue to declare that the Presence of God's All-perfection, All-wisdom, and All-presence is the only Power working in the lives of my loved ones this day and every day!

And So It Is!

10

Living The Life That You Desire

Author's note: The following lesson has been personally worked with and divinely interpreted from the truth of the teachings of Christ, which reveal the following realities of our Divine Selfhood.

The pure and sincere desires of your heart are the divine desires of the Heart of God, desiring to be made manifest in your life if these desires are truly pure, sincere, and desiring of the best for all concerned.

Ask for, and desire, that which is pure and upright, and it shall be given to you. Seek for, and genuinely desire, divine fulfillment in your life, and you shall find that God's fulfillment is already yours. Knock at the door of your heart center with faithful desire and the Presence of God will be made known to you. Everyone that asks for and desires truth will receive truth; and everyone that seeks and desires the Will of God finds God's Will being done in their lives.

With every desire that you have, desire to do the perfect Will of God and if you are sincere, you can be assured that all of the desires of your heart will be the perfect, divine desires of God being made manifest in your daily life experience.

Through the pure desires of your heart, the truth of God will be made known to you. And the truth is: God Desires and Wills that you have life and that you have it more abundantly.

Many, if not most, of the experiences that you experienced yesterday, and in the past, were created out of the dominant desires and attitudes that you held within yourself of how yesterday was going to be—and that is how your yesterday turned out being. *It is that simple.* The majority of your experiences that you are experiencing today are being created from the dominant desires, hopes, wishes, fears, and attitudes that you are *now holding* within your mind and heart of how today is going to be—and that is your today. *It is that simple.* So now I will ask you to ask yourself sincerely and honestly—*How do you want your tomorrow to be?* The way, in which you truly believe, within the desire of your heart that influences your emotional attitude, that your tomorrow will turn out is, to a great degree, the way in which your tomorrow will unfold. *It is that simple.*

From time to time in our lives, it is important that we put ourselves first, take some quiet time, and ask ourselves the following questions honestly and sincerely.

> *What spiritual qualities do you desire to feel within the innermost center of your heart at this time in your life? Which divine principles and laws do you desire to prove as a living reality in this lifetime that you are living? What kind of person do you really desire to become spiritually? Do you desire more integrity of character and spiritualized self-confidence? Do you desire to have a greater sense of inner and outer harmony? Do you desire to know what it feels like to live in an inner atmosphere of unconditional love the majority of the time? What do you really desire?*

Whatever you really desire within your spiritualized mind and heart—that is what you will begin to create. *It is that simple.*

Each and every one of us truly desires to live a life that is personally rewarding so that we can feel worthwhile and productive. We all desire and deserve to live a life wherein we feel that we are successful in our ability to express our unique talents to the world around us. Each of us desires and needs to live a life that is free from disruptive and paralyzing emotional pain, and to live a life that is filled with the rewards of loving, trusting, and nurturing relationships. In other words, we all have a spiritually-ordained desire to live a life of abundant, radiant, energy-giving joy, usefulness, and aliveness.

We are each born with an internalized, *intuitive desire nature that* seeks to live an inner life wherein we are absolutely aware of our personal and spiritual wholeness. We have an inherent, *intrinsic desire nature that* yearns to live a life where we are inwardly assured of our God-given ideal of eternal prosperity and well-being. In the depth of our creative soul nature, we naturally and instinctively desire to live a life that is full of unfettered and endless creative expression so that we can give to this world something of greatness. In reality, we all have a, *spiritually-inherited desire nature*, which aspires to live a life that has real meaning, a life filled with absolute unconditional love, and daily-uninterrupted harmony. This essential desire, for productivity, health, and wholeness in all areas of our life experience, is the natural desire of the truth of our divinity seeking expression in our everyday lives. This inner and personal desire for completeness leads us to the realization of spiritualized truth that knows that—

- Within the Mind, Heart, and Creative Process of God, the Creator of this universe, the Creator of every living being, there is held, at all times, the completed image of your perfect life reality.

Within the truths and practices of this lesson, we will reacquaint ourselves with the *divine image of perfection* that God has in store for us through the vehicle of our desires or *spiritualized-personal desire nature*. When our human desires are elevated to a higher level of spiritual consciousness, we are then assured that we can use the *personal desires of our heart, of our inner soul,* as a powerful tool for the concrete manifestation of our own personal *Heaven on Earth*. When you sincerely desire, *daily,* to join with the Presence of God within your mind and heart, and there to truly desire and seek that God's will be done in you and through you, then you can be assured that your personal desires are the *Divine Desires of God* being expressed through your *spiritualized-desire nature*.

Throughout this lesson you will embark on the exciting journey of knowing what it is that God has in store for you this day, this year, and this lifetime. If you completely release from your mind all of your personal, preconceived ideas of lack and limitation and join with the Mind of God which is wholly filled with thoughts of abundance, and join with the *Will of God* which only desires for you absolute fulfillment, then you will be filled to over-flowing with rich ideas, enthusiastic understanding, and visions of joy within your personal mind, heart, and life.

YOUR FULFILLMENT ALREADY IS!

You will be living the life that you truly desire in proportion to your ability to cultivate a personal awareness that consistently knows that—

- Within the Mind, within the Heart, within the Creative Consciousness of God, your complete fulfillment already exists.

Throughout the following lesson, you will find practices to work with which will help you to become a clearer instrument, through which the desires of God and the desires of your heart can join together to *divinely co-create* a life that is absolutely extraordinary! Included within the following teaching is a process through which you will easily and clearly recognize that the dominant desires, wishes, and beliefs, which you hold within your personal creative consciousness, bring into manifestation the daily experiences that you have.

The creative power of allowing the fulfillment of God into your life is mainly brought about through your feelings of appreciation, gratitude, and unconditional love for what you already have—together with having an expectant enthusiasm for the wonders that God has already prepared for you, which you have yet to experience. To be free within yourself, to be a clear and divine instrument through which the creative power of God's fulfillment can be brought about through your ability to continually feel enthusiastic appreciation, gratitude, and unconditional love, you must free yourself of all negativity that may still be within your consciousness. Following are *Principles* and *Practices,* which will help you to fully free yourself of all negativity, thus allowing and bringing forth the perfect creations of God into your daily life experience.

MORNING MEDITATION PRACTICE
RELEASING OF ALL NEGATIVITY

For three to five minutes *join with* and *rest in* oneness with the Presence of God within your heart-center. Feel the unconditional caring love that God has for you now, and at all times. Feel the supreme peace that fills you when you know that you are truly loved and cared for by God the supreme Creator of all life and substance. Feel the oneness between yourself and the Presence of God's supportive love for you and your life within the pure and immaculate core of your heart. And then *rest further* into the emotional atmosphere of God's eternal and absolute love. *Rest further* into a deeper reality of inner peace. *Rest further* into an acceptance of oneness with the Presence of God.

With your body relaxed and your mind and heart joined together—

- Fully and completely release all ideas that you have about the day ahead.

- Feel your mind empty of all thoughts and planning about the day ahead.

- Let your heart grow open with the letting go of all anxious emotions.

Rest in this state of emptiness and stillness for three to five minutes. Feel and accept the peace—sense and experience the letting go—savor the inner joy—come home to your special relationship with the Presence of God within your own beingness, fully and completely.

Now sincerely, slowly, silently, and repeatedly say to yourself for five to fifteen minutes—

- God—I am now an empty pure vessel for you to fill.

As you slowly repeat this statement of spiritual truth to your inner self-reality—

- Feel the thoughts of God fill your mind. Let the All-Knowing Mind of God fill you with the reality of who you are as a vessel that is eagerly waiting to be filled with your God-Self-Reality.

- Feel the love, the joy, and the peace of God fill your heart until you are so overwhelmed with these divine feelings of ecstasy that you know, without any question, that you are far above feeling the every-day, mundane emotions of this world.

- Rest in this beautiful state of inner fulfillment—then slowly join the world being fully equipped with your Divine God Ideas for this day.

Visualization Exercise—

Whenever you find yourself in need of making a decision, take a moment of stillness and picture your mind as an empty, divine container, into which God's Will and Wisdom are filling you with the answer or answers that you are seeking, so that you are living a completely fulfilled life.

Note: Your answer or answers may very well be revealed to you as an inner peaceful and expectant desire. This desire will be a desire that God has for you. This desire will be a divine desire from the Heart of God Who desires that you have absolute freedom from all forms of lack and limitation.

Presence of God Exercise—

Periodically during the day, take a few minutes of inner quietness and feel the Presence of God filling you with divine wisdom, unconditional love, eternal peace, and a feeling of joy without any restrictions.

Evening Healing Exercise—

Every evening, before you go to sleep, let go of all of the concerns of this day and the next. In a state of emotional and mental serenity, intentionally know that God's Wisdom, God's Ideas, God's Guidance, and God's Love will fill your whole being, while you are sleeping, to bring to you over-all healing for the day ahead.

Evening Exercise—

If you have a decision to make, or you are unsure of what to do with a certain aspect of life—ask the All-Knowing Presence of God within your mind and heart to reveal the right answer, the right direction, or the understanding that you are seeking before you go to sleep. Many times the All-Knowing wisdom of God can reach us easier during our sleep time because our conscious thoughts of negativity and fear are not as active. In this way, God can speak to your mind and heart through the symbolism of your dreams, or through the calm clarity of your mind when you first awaken in the morning. Be sure to keep a pen and paper nearby so that you can write down all of the inspirations that you receive during the highly creative time of your sleep and awakening.

> *Following, are the spiritual principles of truth that you will want to contemplate and work with within your thoughts and awareness so that you become a clearer vessel for the truth of God to demonstrate through. There is a specific divine principle with which to work. Be sure to contemplate the daily divine principle throughout the day. Be alert to any divine revelations that come to your mind during the day.*

PRINCIPLES TO FOLLOW AND WORK WITH DAILY

For The Outer Demonstration
of
Your Inner Spiritual Desires

Day One—Principle One

• To some extent, today is the product of your own limited, humanly distorted, and spiritually untrue view of yourself and your life, which is usually filled with some emotional and mental negativity. Now is the time to empty yourself of any negative programming from the past and allow yourself to be filled with the positive, demonstrative power of appreciation and gratitude for your own divinity and for the sacredness of your own life.

• Now is the time to let go of every thought of limitation about yourself and your life and be completely filled with spiritually-energized appreciation and gratitude for the All-good and perfection, which is held within the Consciousness of God, specifically for you, and express this in your daily life experience.

Exercise—Start your morning by taking a few quiet, introspective minutes to yourself and imagine that this is literally the first day of your life. Imagine that you have been reborn during your sleep, with the full knowledge and the full illumination of who you are spiritually. You are now born into a new life where you know, without a single disbelief, that you are spiritually perfect, whole, and complete! You know that the clear and gentle voice of God's All-Knowing divine wisdom is continually guiding you through this new day and that you are filled with divine intelligence. You are filled with exciting and joyous hope for you have all the guidance, self-confidence, and love that you have need of because of your illumined relationship with the Presence of God within your mind and heart. Now go about your new day being the spiritualized-truth of who you really are, which is a divine representation of the All-Knowing wisdom and illumination of God!

Advanced Exercise—At the conclusion of your morning meditative realization of your true and new divine state of personal perfection, take a quiet introspective moment to yourself to spiritually contemplate the following questions. Honestly ask the innermost center of your heart, your spiritualized desire nature, which is now intentionally and lovingly joined with the Heart, the spiritualized *Desire Nature* of God—

• **If I now really know** that I am made in the perfect image and likeness of God—If I really know that I am now free of all negative thoughts, emotions, beliefs, and images of myself as somehow being less than spiritually perfect—If I really know that I am the most blessed of divine instruments for the full glory of God to express through—*How do I now feel within the center of my emo-*

tional being, and what inner image of myself does this spiritualized feeling and emotion take?

List your divinely perceived image of spiritualized perfection below so that you have a spiritualized, divinely perceived *emotional-feeling image* within yourself that you can focus on, remind yourself of, and live throughout the day.

- -

- -

For Example—Perhaps you are now filled with the spiritualized-emotional feelings of being completely one with the pure perfection of God. You are now filled entirely with the inner feeling of completeness within yourself because of your oneness with the Presence of God, which has just been intuitively revealed to you through your open and purely positive heart-center. You feel an absolute knowingness within your heart-center of an inner sense, or reality, of sureness about your divine relationship with the Presence of God, in which there is no longer any feeling of separation.

This divine revelation, or personal experience of union with the Presence of God, has now taken form as an internal image within yourself of one who is completely sure of their divinity, in their moment-to-moment working partnership with the Presence of God. You now have an inner image of yourself as being definitely one with the Presence of God within yourself, which you now know as a concrete living experience.

You have just seen, first hand, the divine truth of your inseparable relationship with the living Presence of God, which resides within your heart, mind, and soul. You have just felt and literally experienced what it feels like to know God on an intimate and personal level. Now you are ready to live the divinely-revealed *feeling or image* of God's Presence living within you and through you throughout the entire day and throughout eternity!

Further Explanation—

The emotional-feeling-image that you have just perceived is an image of perfection that has communicated itself from the Heart of God to your heart. This incredible experience of spiritual truth has had the chance to be known and perceived within yourself, very simply, because you have taken the time to empty yourself of all negative images, and you have intentionally desired from your pure heart-center to be made new and whole within your own consciousness by join-ing with, and communicating with, the Consciousness of God which is always conscious of your divine perfection. You now have a divinely-perceived and expe-rienced *spiritualized-emotional-image* of the spiritual truth of who you are. This spiritualized-emotional-image of your divinity is a living energy image of perfec-tion that you can continue to live with and act out from throughout your life from now on.

During the day continue to remind yourself of what it feels like to be living within the divine image that you experienced, which was revealed to you from the Heart of God during your morning meditation. Continue to bring this important divine revelation of your divine reality of perfection into greater reality by desiring to be, and to live, this image of perfection with your whole heart, mind, and soul.

This is an exercise that you can use and grow from throughout your entire life! As time goes by, as you keep track of the personal divine revelations that you have received (in a spiritual journal), you will find that the divine images that you receive daily will continue to expand. The reason your image of yourself expands is because your capacity to see yourself as God sees you will become more readily available to you as you continue to desire to be the perfection that God has cre-ated you to be. Your images of yourself as being somehow limited will be healed and lessened as you continue to free yourself of all of the limiting thoughts and emotions that you have about yourself that are negative in nature. The Con-sciousness of God is infinite and unlimited; therefore, your capacity to express unlimited, infinite, and forever-expanding images of perfection is also without limit or boundaries!

Day Two—Principle Two

If, when you meditate, you can let go of your humanly-limited personal will suf-ficiently so that your very mind and heart can be filled with the thoughts, will, and the desires of God, then your personal life will be one of true and lasting inner happiness and satisfaction, and emotional pain will leave your life forever.

Today's Affirmation—

- Today I desire to be the instrument through which God expresses God's divine feelings of happiness and satisfaction.

Exercise—Today, desire to let go completely of any sense of your personal limited will being done, a personal will that may be filled with a false sense of sadness, depression, and a lack of satisfaction about yourself and your life. Let the divine desire, the divine *Will of God* fill you with feelings of happiness and contented satisfaction throughout the whole day.

Whether you realize it or not, the human personal will is either consciously or unconsciously filled with false thoughts and feelings of a negative nature. And even within the most positive of humans wills, there still is a limited picture of the miracles that are waiting for us to accept into our lives. Thus, it is through the intentional letting go completely of the human personal will, and desiring to allow the Divine *Will of God* to work through us, that we become a pure instrument for the miracle-working power of the creative Consciousness of God to create through.

Advanced Exercise—As you awaken in the morning, take a few minutes of meditation to join with the Presence of God within your mind and heart. Sincerely and freely let go of, and surrender, your human will to God. Surrender all of the desires that you have about how this day should be. Surrender all of the desires that you have about how you want to feel. Surrender all of the desires that you have about how your life should be lived. Surrender all that you feel that you have need of to be happy and inwardly satisfied. Become empty and at peace, desiring nothing at all, needing nothing at all, and be in inner peace.

Work With the Following Spiritual Practices During the Day

Ask the Presence of God within you to influence every word that you speak, within yourself to yourself. Let the words that you speak to yourself be words of happiness about who you are and about the life that you are living. Enthusiastically desire that every word that you speak outwardly is the unlimited happiness of God speaking through you. Know that you have completely let go of any desire to speak forth words of gloom and doom. Know that it is the *Will of God* that you be the instrument through which the happiness of God is spoken forth.

Desire to be filled all day long with the positive thinking Mind of God that is continually thinking thoughts of satisfaction and contentment about the universe of perfection that God has already created. Desire to join with the Mind of God that knows that all that has been created is very good! Desire to elevate your every thought to the level of joining with the *Divine Thoughts of God*, Who thinks only thoughts of this universe as being created from unconditional love.

Intentionally let go of your human will that falsely wills to think thoughts of a limiting and negative nature. Desire that the *unrestricted Will of God* think through you at all times. Know that *God Wills* that you think with a mind that is illumined with the creative thoughts of God.

Personally desire to think about, and acknowledge, the wonderment of God's perfect creations all day long! Think only thoughts that create an inner sense of happiness and satisfaction. Think about how happy you are that you desire to be the supreme happiness of God in expression. Think about how happy you are to be filled with the *Will of God* Who wills that you be continually living in a state of supreme happiness!

Desire to be united with the Heart of God Who feels only happiness and satisfaction about the daily life that you are living. Let the full expression of the happiness of God live through you this day! Let go of any sense of a human personal will that falsely feels that it cannot be happy because of this problem, or this disagreeable person, and so on. Remember that God does not recognize any reason to be less than happy. God is the one power, and the only power of unconditional love, and there is no other power to oppose that reality of love. Thus, God is continually in a feeling state of divine happiness and contentment. Desire to be filled with the *Will of God*, knowing that it is the *Will of God* to continually feel, express, and experience happiness to the fullest through you this day and every day!

Live this day as one who is in constant inner communion and communication with the Presence of God. Let yourself be completely free from any personal fear-based thoughts, concerns, and worries, and let God fill you with an inner sense of happiness, inner satisfaction, and eternal contentment that is not dependent on any outside condition. Realize that you in your conscious oneness with God's Presence are the only true source of happiness and satisfaction. Realize that all true happiness and serenity comes from within yourself first, from within your inner conscious awareness, and then is expressed outwardly through your feelings of happiness and contentment. At the conclusion of your meditational practice, commit yourself to feeling and expressing the inner consciousness of happiness and satisfaction all day long, no matter what!

In the Morning—be sure to remember to commit yourself to feeling an inner sense of happiness all day long. Really allow yourself to inwardly feel happy because you know that you are one with God's Presence Who desires for you complete happiness and fulfillment within yourself and within your life.

Intentionally, and alertly realize during the day, that God's will for you is that you have and experience complete happiness, and that you have absolute freedom from all lack and limitation. Calmly know that God's will for you is greater than any will for good that you could desire for yourself. Many times, we, in our clouded awareness, have no idea what it is that would make us truly happy, but God does!

Day Three—Principle Three

This universe is being lived by one great vibration of the *Desire of God* living out God's reality in manifest form. This manifest form, this universe, your world, your body, and God's livingness of you—is perfect.

Today's Affirmation—

• Today I desire to be the vehicle through which the Presence of God is experiencing life through me and through my life.

Exercise—Today, joyously and in anticipation of unlimited miracles happening, let God live through you to the fullest. Let the *greatest possibility thinker* in the world run, guide, and create your day. Know that you are the expression, the example, the teacher of *God's Divine Fulfillment* made manifest to the immediate world around you.

Advanced Exercise—Before you start your day, imagine that you and your life are being lived by the Presence of God expressing through you. Realize that you are the instrument through which the Presence of God, within your mind and heart, is expressing, experiencing, and feeling all positive emotions. Realize that your life is the vehicle through which the Presence of God is also experiencing the positive life.

Take a special, sacred moment to really know that you are the instrument through which the *Divine Desire* of God wishes to express positive emotions. Sit quietly and open your heart fully to the *positive emotion(s) that God desires to express through you* at this time in your life. Allow The Presence of God within your heart center to communicate to you the main positive emotion that God feels that you have need of at this time to make your life a greater miracle. Ask God—

- What main positive emotion do You desire to express through me this day?

As you allow yourself to really listen to the *positive emotion(s)* that God desires for you to make your own, and experience and express on a consistent basis, you are literally in a co-creative partnership with God. You are now ready to live the emotionally perfect life that God created you to live. As you become aware of *the main positive emotion that God desires* for you to manifest, as you listen to God speaking to your heart, list your impressions below so that you will be able to remind yourself of these important revelations each day. I would also suggest that you work often with this exercise and that you keep your personal revelations in a private notebook.

For Example—Does God desire that you be completely free from all personal feelings that you may have of being one who is not good enough, or worthy enough, or talented enough to be an instrument through which God is expressing God's Presence perfectly? If so, then you now know that God desires you to be your true, spiritually-ordained magnificent perfection. God desires that you feel and express a sense of reverence and honor towards yourself because you are the divine instrument through which God is expressing! You also know that the Presence of God will help you to realize this great truth about yourself if you but meet God halfway, by acknowledging God's desire for your perfection, and then joining with this same desire for perfection within your own heart.

- Each morning as you first awaken, take a moment, feel the unconditional love that God has for you, and from your heart-center intuitively ask—

  Today, the unconditionally loving Heart of God desires that I feel, do, be, and emotionally express_____(what positive emotion)_____.

- Or

  Divine Presence of God—What main positive emotion do You desire to express through me this day?

- Or

  Divine Presence of God—How do You desire to express your positive emotions through me this day?

Three Ways to Get in Touch with The Desire Nature of God

- Intuitively, with an inner listening attitude, ask the Presence of God within your heart-center how God desires to feel, to express, through you this day—through one major emotion or feeling. (As described in the above exercise.)

- Discerningly look within your emotional life at this time and intuitively ask yourself—How does my own soul desire to feel this day, what does my own heart yearn to feel?

  For Example—Your own soul or heart may desire to feel a deep inner sense of appreciation for yourself. Thus, you would work on knowing that the Presence of God expressing through you desires that you express greater appreciation for your true God-Self, and have a greater appreciation for the Presence of God living in you and through you.

- Intuitively ask yourself what negative emotion you are feeling in the morning that is keeping you from feeling good about yourself and about your life. Define this negative emotion and realize that it represents an opposite positive emotion that you need to express and make your own living reality.

  For Example—You may feel a negative feeling of dread about the day before you. As you intuitively look at and define this negative emotion, you clearly see that the opposite emotional expression that you are in need of is the emotion of unconditional enthusiasm for your life. Now you are aware that you need to allow the enthusiastic expression of the unrestricted life of God to express through you fully and completely!

Note: This exercise is an extremely important way to become intuitively aware of God's divine guidance for you. When you let go of your personal desires and you ask the Presence of God within your heart to reveal the *Divine Desires* that God has for you and your life, then your heart is in communion with the Heart of God. I wholeheartedly suggest that you ask yourself these questions every morning of your life and that you keep a record of your answers, which you can use for divine guidance on a daily basis, and also for divine guidance in the future.

Realize fully during the day that you and God are absolutely One and all that God is, you are, and all that you are and all that you experience, God is also aware of and experiencing. Look at every moment, look at every experience that you have today with the *Eyes of God, Who see only perfection.*

Day Four—Principle Four

As you step back and let God, within your mind and heart, re-form your attitude about yourself and your life, in proportion, you will see miracles start to happen each and every day.

Today's Affirmation—

- Today I desire to live within God's divine law of individual and universal harmony.

Exercise—Today, gratefully know that God is *now* filling your heart and mind with thoughts and feelings of complete harmony and healing for all areas of yourself and your life.

Advanced Exercise—As you go about your activities, concentrate on, and hold onto, the inner knowing that knows that God is a Presence that is with you all of the time during the day and night. Know that it is God's Presence that is continually keeping your emotional state filled with a deep and abiding sense of inner harmony and well being. Whenever you sense any feeling, any thought, or any outer activity that may attempt to take away your God given reality of harmony—instantly give the discordant feeling, thought, or situation to the Presence of God that is within you to heal. Do not worry about how it will be healed, just let it go to the divine intelligence of God to heal—thus keeping yourself in a state of harmony continuously throughout the day and night.

Never forget that divine harmony is your spiritual reality, and that anything that appears to take your divine harmony from you, is just an illusion of lack of harmony waiting to be healed and dissolved by the truth of harmony!

Day Five—Principle Five

Every day is a divine opportunity to let God live through your personal nature to bring about the right re-creation of your daily life experience, which is one that will be filled with all that you have ever hoped for. It is God's plan, it is God's will for you, to live in the conscious reality of fulfillment that gives you the freedom to express your true nature, which is one of unconditional and unrestricted joy and aliveness.

Today's Affirmation—

- Today I desire to express my best self to this world through my personal ability to communicate unconditional joy and boundless, unrestricted aliveness.

Exercise—Today, let God use you as an instrument of joy and aliveness. Gratefully accept that you are a healing agent to those around you who are in need of more joy and aliveness in their lives.

Advanced Exercise—The spiritualized emotions of unconditional joy and unrestricted aliveness are highly creative in nature. Whenever you feel joyful and alive, you are expressing your best self to others. These times of joy and aliveness are being expressed because you feel really good about yourself and about your life. Freely experiencing and expressing the feelings of goodness, joy, and aliveness is the way that your life is to be lived each and every day. It is from your internalized feeling of joy and aliveness that you create your personal outer expression of enchantment about life, ecstasy for living, and energetic enthusiasm for life.

In the morning, connect with the divine source of joy and aliveness within yourself by dedicating every moment of this day to the goodness or glory of God. Allow the All-intelligence of God to create your day through the expression of your own joy and aliveness. Refuse to allow any negative emotions and thoughts from yourself or others stand in the way of your divine right to be, and express freely, your own unique expression of joy and aliveness! Watch to see how others around you tend to resonate to these wonderful creative qualities.

Day Six—Principle Six

Let the Presence of God live through you by dedicating yourself to being the instrument through which God expresses God's Self as your unique personality.

Today's Affirmation—

- Today I desire to be one with the literal Presence of God uniquely expressing through me as me.

Exercise—As you awaken, dedicate yourself to living this day *as if* the very Presence of God was living through you, as you.

Advanced Exercise—Today, let God live through you in every feeling that you feel—in every word that you speak—and in every activity that you perform. Acknowledge the fact, consistently during the day, that you are now filled with a real inner sense of serenity and wholeness about who you are, which nothing of this world can ever take from you.

- With every feeling that you feel—ask yourself—Is this the way that God would feel about this person or situation?

Now you are joining with and allowing the Presence of God to express through your emotional nature within the everyday activities of your life! You are intuitively listening to how God wants to heal you and others through the vehicle of your unique emotional nature!

- With every word that you speak either outwardly or internally—ask yourself—Are these words that I am about to speak the words that God would speak to this person or in this situation?

Now you are definitely expressing your divinity by knowing that it is the power, truth, and absolute knowingness of God, which is speaking through you! You are literally a *divine spokesperson of God's absolute truth.* God is using you to speak spiritual truth, so that others in your life are helped!

- In every activity that you perform—ask yourself—Am I doing what God would be doing in this situation?

Now you are literally allowing God to perform God's truth and miracles through you and through your life!

Day Seven—Principle Seven

It is very simple and easy to live your life the way that you desire it to be. All you need do is to turn over the control of your life to the Presence of God. Remember that the Presence of God always desires for you greater love, greater happiness, greater fulfillment, and greater success than you could ever desire or envision for yourself! The Presence of God desires to live through you, to bring to you the awareness of a day that is beautiful, in perfect divine order, and enriched every moment. So … what do you desire this day?

The Supreme divine Principle to remember as you are working with this lesson is—

- Within the Heart, within the Consciousness of God, your perfect day, your perfect life always exists. For the Heart of God, the Consciousness of God can only behold perfection, and it is out of this universal perfection that all of life is created.

Exercise—Take this special day and look at your life as God sees it and ask yourself—

- If the Presence of God was literally living this day through me, how would I perceive this day? How would I feel about any discordant situation? What would my attitude be about all so-called lack and limitation? Would God feel lack or limitation within the abundant universe of God's creating? Of course not!

Define, in words that have real meaning to you, how the perfect *Creative Consciousness* of God desires your life to be lived as a life that is free from all false beliefs of lack and limitation. Define how *God Desires* for you to be living each day with a life of boundless health, unconditional abundant love, confidant God-Self expression, and unlimited prosperity. Define your life as a life that God is living through you—a life that is effortlessly in the flow of God's divine law of ever-present fulfillment and list below.

- _

- _

- _

- _

Take the above *divinely-ordained definition of your life*, write it on a card, and put it in places where you will be reminded of its magnificent truth often during the day. Each day, remind yourself of this divinely-perfect life that you desire to be living, and let the supreme desire nature of God express and create perfection in your life now.

Second advanced Exercise—Within an inner contemplative state ask yourself the following question—

• What major lack or limitation stands in the way of my living the life that I and the Presence of God within me desires to live?

List the intuitively perceived lack or limitation that is in need of transformation.

• _

• _

• _

• _

Now realize that that false sense of perceived lack or limitation needs to be replaced with the truth of unlimited fulfillment that you and God desire to demonstrate in your life at this time, ***and list or affirm*** in your own personal and unique words of energized truth.

• _

• _

• _

• Now embrace, comprehend, and continue to affirm and realize that the desire of God, the *Will of God* for you is to live a life that is free from all lack and limitation!

For Example—Let's say that you intuitively perceive that you falsely believe that your life is limited because you are not expressing the full talent that you have within yourself for writing books, articles, screenplays, or novels, which others will benefit from and enjoy, and for which publishers will pay highly. Thus, you are falsely holding back your own creative talents and the creative talent of God expressing through you, plus you are also limiting your income and limiting your ability to make a good living doing something that you love.

Adamantly take that false belief, deliberately let it go, and decide not to give it any power by refusing to give it any more attention either through your thoughts, beliefs, emotions, or actions. Just as a plant would wither and die if not watered, so will your false beliefs of limitation wither and die if you refuse to water them with your mental and emotional attention!

Then take the time and effort that is necessary to become an instrument through which the creative genius of God's Presence expresses through you. Continually remember that within the Heart and Consciousness of God, you already are highly talented in specific areas of expression. God created each one of us as a unique expression of one special and specific, if not many, talents that God desires to express through us. This is true not only for our own enrichment but also for the enrichment and enjoyment of others with whom we may have contact or influence. Take a stand, be brave and adventurous, be a divine vessel through which the beauty and eternal grandeur of God is made manifest, in this lifetime!

In Conclusion

Take this day to really change your attitude and perception about yourself and your life. What you desire this day, and day after day, becomes the pattern of your life. This day, desire to accept your life as a majestic gift that God created for you from the unconditionally loving Heart of God. Be one with the divine creative intelligence that created all that is which is contained within this infinite universe! This infinite universe is your home. This day, desire to be in a state of joyful living within this eternal home, within the heart of God, in which you live and move and have your being.

978-0-595-43118-2
0-595-43118-6